Control Tactics Instructor Manual

Control Tactics Instructor Manual

Tom Gillis

Tom Gillis
2016

Copyright © 2016 by FTS Inc.

All rights reserved. This book or any portion thereof may not be reproduced or used in any manner whatsoever without the express written permission of the publisher except for the use of brief quotations in a book review or scholarly journal.

First Printing: 2016

ISBN 978-0-9939421-5-0

Tom Gillis
118 Cimarron Grove Road
Okotoks Alberta Canada T1S 2H1

www.ftsma.com

Ordering Information:

Special discounts are available on quantity purchases by corporations, associations, educators, and others. For details, contact the publisher at the above listed address.

U.S. trade bookstores and wholesalers: Please contact FTS Inc. Tel: (403) 829-7897or email info@ftsma.com

Dedication

To all of the unsung heroes who work on the Law Enforcement Spectrum. Thank you for your selfless untiring service.

Table of Contents

Forward 11

Training Methodology and Tactical Priorities 15

Interpersonal Communication 25

Use of Force 31

Mechanical Restraint Application and Searching 37

Edged Weapon Defense 45

Pressure Points and Facilitation Targets 51

Control Holds 57

Oleoresin Capsicum Spray 63

Baton Use 69

Takedowns 75

Inside Position Combatives 81

Ground Fighting 87

Strikes 101

Weapon Retention and Disarming 107

Written Exam Answer Sheet 107

Blank Written Exam 123

Blank Practical Exam 129

References 133

Forward

In the past forty years or so I have invested an immense amount of my life educating myself about the world of police defensive tactics. Being a police officer (from FTO to chief), a trainer, and police writer this topic is important not only to me but to those I work with. Often times, it is the difference between a good night and tragic one. As the years flew by I have also found it is not the street fight you must survive but the administrative and legal battles that loom. So this quest is not only to understand defensive tactics, but also the applicable laws in their judicious use. To study this topic it is more than reading or watching demonstrations on video. Many of an hour was spent on the mat in sweat equity seeking its true applications. Several demonstrations and lectures were by this book's author as a matter of fact.

Tom made a lasting impression with me during his first presentation. His methodology of teaching was all inclusive. All who attended were respected and taught, no one was excluded from the presentation. Most all defensive tactics systems have influences from the martial arts side of the house which often convolutes the teaching of it to the masses. Of course there are some who will reject martial arts teachings as nearly witchcraft. Others get confused or disinterested upon the first mention of a foreign word or concept. Tom never let that occur; he kept the highest degree marital artist as interested as the first time rookie officer attendee. I found this very important for he did not seek the comfort of a fellow marital artist. Nor did he toady up to fellow more skilled instructors, all students came to learn and they did.

In conversation over dinner one night while we were attending the International Law Enforcement Educators and Trainers Association (www.ileeta.org), I challenged Tom to begin writing. His impressive instructional skills coupled with his commitment to his students should shine through so therefore nothing but good could from his efforts. So since I challenged him to this quest, it only seems fitting that he asked that I do his forward.

This book will give especially our Canadian colleagues great insights for it is an all-inclusive work. This is not only a how to, why it works but also a legal application of the process. Recall I mentioned you often have to have legal and administrative survival as well? Since Tom is based in Alberta, Canada his legal references are based in the Canadian legal system. Although a different country, still many similarities can be used within the United States or any place for that matter. Common sense is universal.

In the world of law enforcement, security, corrections and self-defense there is a gambit of police defensive tactics systems. Some more applicable to your station in life than others, you are often left pondering on how this system will fit your needs. I recall that Miyamoto Musashi (1584-1645), historical swordsman and rōnin, made it his life's study of other systems (way) to fully understand tactics. If this tactician did this, then we should consider it as well. This book will give you application of each procedure with examples. I am particularly impressed with the photography, which at first blush may appear mundane to the photographic set but again the logic behind the concept is brilliant. Too many books have nearly cartoon characters, some have the depictions in karate gis and some in uniforms. Again, the plain inclusiveness of the photography is subtle and does not create the air of neither elitism nor exclusion. This is the way Tom teaches and now presents his work, in that every student counts.

William L. "Bill" Harvey

Module 1. Training Methodology and Tactical Priorities

It is crucial that before learning physical techniques participants have a firm understanding on the 6 Tactical Priorities during an incident and how to care for themselves after an incident. These are fundamentals that participants will be encouraged to develop during their skill development and continue to practice once operational.

Chapter Testing Objectives

1. Explain the Blue Guardian Training Methodology
2. List and describe the 6 Tactical Priorities during contact with subject's
3. List and describe 3 considerations for action after a critical incident
4. Demonstrate a basic understanding of Post Traumatic Stress Disorder

The goal of this program is to provide Control Tactics Instructors with the knowledge to understand the methodology that went into creating the control tactics system. As will be demonstrated throughout the chapter, the system IS NOT simply a collection of techniques but rather strives to create protectors through a holistic training approach which encompasses mind set as well as physical tactics.

The program is aggressive in its approach in that it seeks to answer questions which are not only difficult to answer but that are controversial in nature.

Training Methodology

Blue Guardian views training physical skills slightly differently than most other service providers. As you can see by the graphic below Physical Techniques ARE NOT the most important priority.

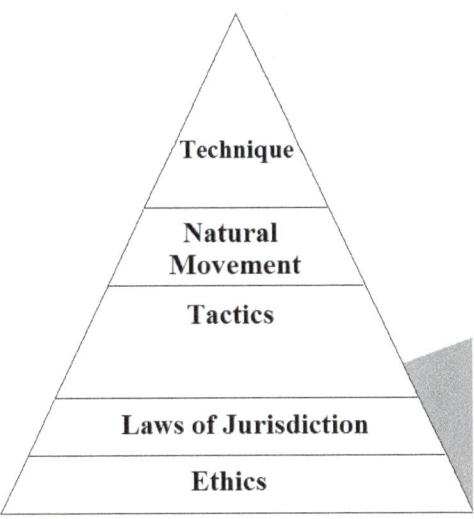

Ethics

As illustrated above the foundation for all Blue Guardian training is **Ethical Behavior**. We maintain that officers must understand that protection of life is their top priority. Ethical behavior means knowing AND doing what's right to protect life. This includes the Officers life, the Publics life, and to do what they can to protect the Subject(s) even in combative situations and definitely post conflict when persons are in their custody. This means that at no time is it acceptable for officers to take any actions that unnecessarily cause harm to any person. This means taking unnecessary risks (i.e. speeding unnecessarily) are not acceptable, and the onus is on them to train their skills to be able to protect life at all times.

This type of training goes beyond just training schema for the typical **perceived stimulus: react** paradigm and focuses on officers being mentally present in all situations and making conscious decisions based on the totality of circumstances. There are many documented cases of officers who received the typical stimulus: react type of training making reasonable mistakes in situations that have caused serious injury and in some circumstances unnecessary death (i.e. BART weapon confusion case). Instead the goal of training should be to instill a sense of **presence** in situations which encourages officers to process and environment and make rapid **conscious** decisions. This level of proficiency takes a lot of work to reach but with hard work and dedication it is possible.

Law

Law Enforcement Officers at all levels have a duty to lead by example by following the laws, rules, regulations, and policies in effect. Blue Guardian focuses on Reasonable and Necessary Use of Force. Remember however that enforcing law cannot violate Ethical Behavior. Trainers and Officers must understand any statutory and case laws in effect in their jurisdiction.

This means that there is an onus on trainers to research, know, and understand the law and be able to transmit it accurately to students. This level of understanding goes far beyond typical Use of Force Models (which aren't law but rather visual representations of law).

For example recent case law indicates that trainers have a responsibility to train officers in their charge in all weapons, at all ranges.

Tactics

Control Defensive Tactics training should teach officers Tactics that are applicable to a variety of situations.

Some examples include (but aren't limited to);

- Shielding and cornering
- Angular Movement
- Changing elevation

- Jamming opponent's attacks before they have time to initiate
- Controlling space
- Engagement and disengagement
- 5 point balance manipulation

Natural Movement

Any physical material taught in a class must follow rules of Natural Movement. This means it is imperative that instructors are constantly evaluating material and asking if what they're teaching violates these rules.

Natural Movement means;

- Legs are responsible for lifting, and moving
- Maintain balance by keeping the head over the hips and back straight
- Limbs don't cross your own center line, and if they do correct it immediately
- When moving joints maintain some flex to avoid lock out and hyper extension
- The less a joint moves the more stable it is (i.e. wrists straight with thumbs up as opposed to twisted with thumbs down)
- Arms push and legs pull
- The body follows the eyes

Technique

When Tactics are combined with Natural Movement in a manner that is Ethical, Legal Techniques are created. Techniques **CANNOT** violate any of the previous levels of development. Techniques that promote the students self discovery and promote a sense of balance, co-ordination, timing, precision, and power are best. A training regime in which techniques build on each other are more desirable than a training program where each technique is different.

When teaching techniques the goal is to teach the student to the point where it exists in the brain stem, and not the pre frontal lobe. Sports science research indicates that an effective way to do this is to limit the amount of time they can work on a piece of material to approximately 20 minutes, take a break from that material, and then come back to it within an hour.

Tactical Priorities

There are 6 tactical priorities that officers should always work on developing in conjunction with their physical skills. In fact in some instances it's the application of these priorities in conjunction within the guidelines of Reasonable Force that will allow officers to decide which tactics or techniques to use. Most officers that are attacked and injured on the job are attacked because they gave the subject the opportunity to hurt them. By using these fundamentals in every contact with subject's you can effectively eliminate some this opportunity.

The Tactical Priorities are;

Priority #1, Don't get hit. Unlike in a combat sport competition, an officer's first priority during any contact with a subject should be to not get struck by that subject. During street altercations there are no rules, no safety equipment, and often no one to help if an officer gets hurt. Subject's can deploy weapons and even in the case of an empty hand altercation officers can't be sure of a subject's intent or if and when they'll stop attacking. For this reason an officer's first priority is to not get hit. The first hit in a street altercation might be the last. There are several tactics an officer can use to maximize their chances of not getting hit;

- **Cover, concealment, and shielding**. Understanding the differences between cover, concealment, and shielding and using them effectively can greatly increase officer safety. Cover is something that will stop the threat from penetrating. It is accepted that something that will stop a bullet is cover. Concealment will allow an officer to hide yourself from the subject but will not stop weapons from penetrating through. A car door in a gun fight is concealment. Remember to move to cover first, and then engage. In non-firearm situations where cover isn't available use items for shielding, such as chairs, tables, and wall corners. Shields provide an obstacle that a subject must navigate to reach the officer but won't stop firearms and doesn't effectively block line of sight to the officer. By using shielding the officer can effectively slow down an attacker providing more time to react.

- **Move on 45, stay alive**. The use of angular movement can move officer's out of the way of incoming attacks and cause the subject to recalculate where the officer is and how to continue an attack. Using 45 degree angular movement relative to a subject can also open opportunities for counter attacks and control techniques.

- **Threat cues.** Often subject's who attack officer's display some threat cues just before the attack. An observant officer will pick up on these threat cues and be prepared to take action. Threat cues include what is said, how it said, eye movement, clenched fists, and other cues of nervousness and anxiety. Don't fall into the trap of focusing on subject's' eyes when talking to them. Watch the hands and the rest of their body/surroundings for threat cues. Officer's who effectively read subject threat cues have been shown to have faster reaction time and in some cases are able to move with a subject's attack instead of after it.

- **Maintain Distance**. Reaction time is defined as the amount of time between when something is observed, processed, a plan formulated, and motor neurons begin to initiate a motor response. Officer's can increase the amount of time they have to complete this process by increasing the distance to a subject. The further the distance from a subject the more time officer's have to react to their actions. This relationship can work against an officer too. If there is too much space from the subject they will have more time to react when physical control is attempted. The minimum distance maintained to a subject should be no less than a step and an arm's reach and greater depending on the situation.

- **Watch for Multiples.** Often time's officer's find themselves faced with multiple opponent's or opponent's with multiple weapons. This of course can be dangerous especially when the officer finds the initial threat, deals with it, and then lowers their guard. For this reason it is important to remember that once a threat is recognized and neutralized to continue to look for others.

- **Keep your hands up.** Always during contact with a subject(s) an officer should remember to keep their hands up. Even if the subject is co-operating and compliant the officers hands should remain above their waste. An easy way to remember this is to index the duty belt. If the subject's actions become somewhat escalated the hands can be raised and used for non-verbal communication at chest or chin level. If an assaultive altercation happens the hands should stay up at face level.

- **De-escalate when available.** The use of professional verbal communication can effectively de-escalate a situation and decrease that chance of injury to the public, the officer, and the subject. When possible communication methods should be developed in training and put into practice. Remember to maintain your professionalism and strive to deescalate situations before they become aggressive. Subject's may try to goad an officer into an altercation by being rude and disrespectful.

- **Disengagement or tactical repositioning.** Disengagement is a tactical consideration that an officer may employ in an attempt to control a situation. If an officer does not have adequate resources to safely control a situation, or if disengagement or tactical repositioning would assist in controlling a situation with a lower level of force, an officer may disengage from the incident. Often disengagement or de-escalation requires an officer to reposition to a tactically sound position and await the arrival of additional resources. Disengagement or tactical repositioning may not be possible in some circumstances. Environmental factors such as obstacles or barriers may physically prevent an officer from adopting these tactics. As well, the distance between the officer and the subject, and the weapon being used by the subject may also eliminate the use of this option. Lastly, the safety of the public and other officers may dictate that disengagement is not an option. Other tactical considerations encompass specialty units and additional resources available to the officer.

    Disengagement is acceptable under 4 conditions.
    1. When there is little to no risk to the public.
    2. When the officer faces death or grievous bodily harm.
    3. When disengaging will **increase** the safety of the public.
    4. When the officer has to disengage to acquire resources or personnel to respond properly to the situation.

Tactical Priority #2, Proactive Actions. Proactive actions mean that the officer must employ techniques to take the initiative and put a subject on the reaction side of the situation. Often officers who find themselves in an assaultive encounter have to wait until after the subject initiates their action. Once an officer has made the determination that force is necessary and what force is reasonable they should be deploying techniques towards the subject. Depending on the circumstances techniques at this stage of the fight generally include stuns, distractions, and strikes. Depending on the totality of circumstances these strikes may be empty handed or armed (i.e. baton, aerosol sprays, conducted energy weapons, less-than-lethal weapons, or firearms).

Tactical Priority #3, Finish the Altercation. To Finish the Altercation an officer uses control methods which limit or eliminate the subject's' ability to continue their illegal or assaultive behavior. Again this will change in any given situation given the totality of the circumstances and it might just be because the subject has lost the intent to resist or fight, perhaps the subject is unconscious or deceased in the case of an application of lethal force. Officers must make a commitment before an altercation to never give up. Every confrontation is <u>winnable</u>. If something isn't working change tactics and continue on. Developing a winning mentality also includes maintenance of equipment, maintaining a high degree of physical fitness, using imagery and visualization during slow times, and finding innovative ways to combat complacency. Remember that complacency is the number one killer of law enforcement officers.

> **It should be noted here that in some instances priorities 1-3 happen simultaneously. For instance if a subject were to produce a knife and lunge at an officer and that officer moves out of the way, produces a side arm, engages with lethal force shooting the subject and the round placement is such that it stops the subject than in that case priorities 1-3 happened together.**
>
> **However the situation unfolds once the subject is unable or unwilling to continue to engage in their resistance or assaultive behavior the officer must continue on to the second part of the priority list. It should be noted that depending on the situation priorities 4-6 might change order. They are provided below in a general format that will fit most situations.**

Tactical Priority #4, Control and arrest. At this stage of an altercation an officer applies mechanical restraints to the subject(s). Depending on the situation an officer may inform the subject of the reason for arrest at this stage and of their rights. At this stage an officer might also complete their search and transport to a holding facility. After successfully arresting/detaining a subject an officer has several responsibilities. The officer will have to prioritize the order in which he carries these out accordingly taking into account the totality of the circumstances.

These responsibilities can be remembered by the acronym **SIS**. This acronym stands for;

Secure the Handcuffs

After placing handcuffs on a subject officer must get in the habit of always securing the handcuffs by using the double lock feature. This is crucial for 3 reasons. First, it helps to prevent subject's from picking the handcuffs and defeating the locking mechanism. Second it insures that the subject can't tighten the handcuffs on purpose to trick the officer into unlocking and loosening them and third once taken into custody a subject's well being is the responsibility of the officer(s). Securing the handcuffs helps protect the subject's hands.

Inform the Subject of the reason for arrest and their rights

Section 29(2) of the Criminal Code of Canada and the Canadian Charter of Rights and Freedoms section 10(a) demands that officers inform the subject of the reason for the arrest or detainment. The officer must inform the subject that they have the right to retain and instruct counsel without delay. This is found under the Canadian Charter of Rights and Freedoms section 10(b). Officers have to inform subject's that they have the constitutional right to remain silent and that any information provided to the officer can and will be used against them in a trial.

Search
According to case law found in *R.v. Warford* officers can conduct a search incident to arrest. When tactically safe to do so follow the procedure outlined in Module 4.

Tactical Priority #5, Call for help. Depending on the lethality of the situation an officer might swap priority 4 and 5. If for instance they or members of the public are injured getting Emergency Services on the way might be more important. In the case of injuries the amount of time from when the injury occurred to when treatment begins can make the difference between life and death. For this reason it's recommended that as soon as tactically possible officers call for help. In the best case scenario this would be before an altercation even began. If however the officer finds themselves surprised that may be impossible.

Tactical Priority #6, Self aid/first aid. As soon as tactically safe to do so officers must check themselves for injuries and then other officers, members of the public, and finally subject's. Although public safety is the number one responsibility in law enforcement any officers present are likely the first responders and will be responsible for treating others. It is impossible for them to treat someone effectively and ongoing before tending to their own wounds.

For this reason each first responder gives themselves and another a primary survey to assess the extent of injury. This process is completed for all members of the public and any subject's involved in the situation and then Emergency Triage and prioritize which injuries get treated accordingly.

Post Incident Priorities

Immediately Following a *Critical Incident* officers should take the consider the following;

1. Call Significant Other. This simple step will ensure the well being of the officers' partner when information gets out by the media and will help calm the officer upon hearing a friendly voice. In the case of single officers any trusted family member or friend should be contacted immediately.

2. Seek Legal Counsel. A well educated lawyer will serve to ensure investigating agencies and officers do not elicit a statement from the involved officers and can help ensure that the officers' legal rights are protected during an investigation.

3. Take 3 days off work. All officers should take a minimum of three days off duty and spend at home. This time allows for memory recovery and helps the officer to examine their own feelings surrounding what transpired during the incident. After this three day period officers are encouraged to return to work and discuss the incident with supervisors and investigating officers and fill out statements and reports. After this period officers involved in a critical incident must watch for signs of *Post Traumatic Stress Disorder* (PTSD) and consult a medical professional if they feel unwell.

The DSM IV provides some guidelines to help us understand PTSD:

1. The person has experienced an event that is outside the range of usual human experience and that would be markedly distressing to almost anyone.

2. The traumatic event is **persistently re-experienced** in at least one of the following ways:
    (1) recurrent and intrusive disturbing recollections of the event
    (2) recurrent distressing dreams of the event
    (3) sudden acting or feeling as if the traumatic event were recurring (includes a sense of reliving the experience, illusions, hallucinations, and flashback episodes, even those that occur upon awakening or when intoxicated)
    (4) intense psychological distress at exposure to events that symbolize or resemble an aspect of the traumatic event, including anniversaries of the trauma

3. **Persistent avoidance** of stimuli associated with the trauma or numbing of general responsiveness (not present before the trauma), as indicated by at least three of the following:
    (1) efforts to avoid thoughts or feelings associated with the trauma
    (2) efforts to avoid activities or situations that arouse recollections of the trauma
    (3) inability to recall an important aspect of the trauma (psychogenic amnesia)
    (4) markedly diminished interest in significant activities (in young children loss of recently acquired
        developmental skills such as toilet training or language skills.
    (5) feeling of detachment or estrangement from others
    (6) restricted feeling of affect, e.g. unable to have loving feelings
    (7) sense of a foreshortened future, e. g. does not expect to have a career, marriage, or children, or a long life

4. **Persistent symptoms of increased arousal** (not present before the trauma), as indicated by at least two of the following:

(1) difficulty falling or staying asleep
(2) irritability or outbursts of anger
(3) difficulty concentrating
(4) hypervigilance
(5) exaggerated startle response
(6) physiologic reactivity upon exposure to events that symbolize or resemble an aspect of the traumatic event (e.g., a woman who was raped in an elevator breaks out in a sweat when entering any elevator)

E. Duration of the symptoms was at least six months after the trauma

> **If, after an altercation, officers are experiencing the above symptoms or any other feeling of being unwell or symptoms that were not present before the incident medical attention should be sought.**

Module 1 Conclusion

Physical Skills Training shouldn't just teach or train physical skills, but rather it should re-enforce *ethical behavior and decision making*, the *laws of jurisdiction*, and *sound tactics* and *body mechanics*. This is often accomplished through learning or practicing *techniques*. Instructors should use smaller blocks of information that are revisited regularly to help keep students mental focus and energy. These mini blocks should be approximately 20 minutes long.

During a control tactics or combat situation following the 6 Tactical Priorities can help officers make good decisions and maximize the safety of the public, the officer(s), and the subject(s). The 6 Tactical Priorities are *Don't Get Hit*, *Proactive Action*, *Finish the Altercation*, *Control and Arrest*, *1st Aid/Self Aid*, and *Call for Help*. Depending on the totality of circumstances the priorities might change order. This framework, along with an understanding of Reasonable Force, can be used to dictate officer responses.

Following an incident there are a few things officers can do to keep themselves safe and healthy. They are *Call a Significant Other*, *Seek Legal Counsel*, and *Take Time Off Work*. Along with these suggestions officers that have been exposed to a traumatic incident should have an understanding of Post Traumatic Stress Disorder and seek medical aid if they're experiencing or think they're experiencing any of the symptoms associated with PTSD.

Module 2. Interpersonal Communication

Communication Skills are possibly the most difficult to develop and should continually be worked on. Poor communication can lead to physical violence whereas excellent communication skills can often de-escalate a situation and resolve conflict before it becomes physical.

Because every situation is different Blue Guardian does not subscribe to the belief that a single script or dialogue can be followed. Instead our method is to understand why people communicate in certain ways and understand how to apply certain principles and concepts to a situation to increase the chance of a non violent outcome. This method allows officers to operate in ways that are comfortable for them and allows for change during rapidly evolving situations.

Chapter Testing Objectives

1. Describe why communication breaks down between people.
2. Describe and demonstrate methods for building rapport and de-escalate verbal conflict.

Understanding why communication breaks down.

Generally speaking people see themselves as intellectual animals capable of reason and logic under all circumstances. This belief however is an illusion. People are emotional animals who use intellect. It is important to understand this difference because during confrontational situations emotion rather than intellect takes over. This is why some people "just don't get it" or can't understand that they're being unreasonable or even dangerous.

Basic communication model

In any verbal conflict there are 3 main components at play. The situation will take form depending on how these components interact. The components are;
    a. What the transmitter thinks they're transmitting
    b. The actual message being transmitted
    c. What the receiver thinks they're receiving

Factors that influence the relationship between these 3 factors are;
- Language barriers of the parties
- Ethnicity
- Religion
- Gender
- State of mind
- Subject matter
- Level of education

- Level of buy-in to the situation
- The medium through which the message is being transmitted

Often what happens is the actual message isn't what either party perceives it to be. The transmitter thinks that they are sending a certain message but the words they're using, the tone and pitch of their voice, and their non-verbal communications are not what they perceive them to be. Body language and non-verbal communication is thought to be responsible for 90% of communication. This means that if someone's body language, tone, pitch, speech rate, etcetera aren't consistent with what they're trying to communicate, confusion and frustration can result.

Likewise due to the receivers' personal circumstances the message gets interpreted upon being received. The receiver interprets the message based on their own circumstances and filter and assigns value to it.

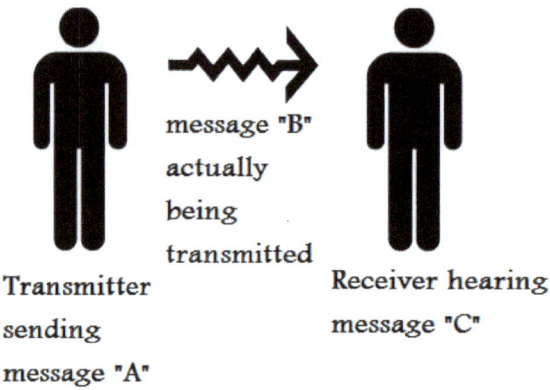

The net result is that neither party are getting what they require in the situation. This cycle can continue back and forth between two unskilled communicators. As the cycle continues emotions increase and even less of the message(s) are received as they were intended.

Due to increased emotions and stress this situation will result in 1 of 2 possible outcomes unless the cycle is broken;

Fight

Both parties become so emotional and frustrated that a physical confrontation ensues between them. This increases chance of injury to both the officer and the subject and the public and increases likelihood of property damage.

Flight

One or both parties become so frustrated by the inability to resolve the issue that they completely shut down and leave the situation. In this case the officer may now be forced into a flight situation or have to initiate physical contact to restrain the subject.

Breaking the cycle

Once this negative communication cycle is understood you can begin to interrupt the cycle at various points to increase the likelihood that communication skills will resolve the situation. Before this can be attempted however a few important points must be remembered. They are;

- Communication skills are as important as physical skills
- Be patient
- Recognize when to switch from communication skills to physical skills
- Evaluate the extent of risk of injury to bystanders, yourself, and the other person as well as risk of property damage when deciding to continue communication skills or switch to physical skills.

Likewise there are communication traps that should be avoided. They are;

- Promising things you're not 100% sure you can deliver
- Threatening action that you're not 100% willing to follow up on
- Using phrases such as "calm down", "relax", "I know what you're going through." Instead officer's can adopt a phrase such as, "I want to help you but I can't understand you right now. Take a few deep breaths and try telling me again."
- Raising voice, putting hands on hips, crossing arms, not looking at subject, glaring at subject, smirking, inappropriate laughter, and other non verbal communications that are disrespectful will create barriers to communication

Breaking the cycle step 1. Create rapport

Rapport is the feeling of being connected between two parties. This is essential in communicating with subject's. People want to feel they're being heard and listened to. The following steps will help officers to build rapport;

- Use positive language and encourage "yes questions". This is accomplished by asking a question that you already know the answer to be yes. An example may be "the property owner asked you to leave and you don't feel that's fair yes?"
- Maintain distance. People are defensive when they feel their personal space is being violated. This is also an important tactic for the officer. A reactionary space of approximately a step and an arm's reach should be maintained at all times.
- Don't stand directly in front of the subject. Not only is this not tactically sound but it also sends a confrontational message. Whenever possible walk in the same direction of a subject off to the side as you're communicating with them. If you can't do that then step just off to one side or the other while still in front of them.
- Demonstrate that you are *Listening* by allowing people to finish sentences without interrupting them. Listen closely for clues about what the person is experiencing or feeling and what they expect for an outcome. Avoid formulating a response in your own mind until the facts have been gathered and confirmed.
- As soon as you notice the subject repeating the same phrase or message over and again recognize that they're trapped in a cycle where they don't feel you've heard them. *Paraphrase* their message back to them and ask them if you got it correct.
- Always keep in mind that this might be a new situation for the subject and they're likely confused and stressed about it. Demonstrate *Empathy* by asking yourself how you'd want to be treated in their shoes.
- *Ask* questions to ascertain the facts AND how people are feeling. Don't assume anything.
- Keep your voice loud and firm but not yelling or rude. Maintain sound tactical body posture. Keep your hands up in front of your chest talking with your hands. Keep moving slightly from side to side or back and forth. This all indicates to a would-be combative person that you're relaxed but ready for escalation. This show of force may deter them from initiating a fight.

Breaking the cycle step 2. Making your sales pitch.

Once rapport is obtained you should change your focus to moving forwards with the purpose of obtaining the other persons involvement. Reinforce that you're interested in a peaceful resolution. If they don't respond positively remind them that fighting will only make the situation worse for everyone involved;

- Remind them that you're not criticising them or who they are but rather your only interest is to resolve the situation.
- Use please and thank and show compassion and respect.

- Try to use the "Law of Reciprocity." This is a human communication law that transcends culture, ethnicity, and religious barriers. The Law of Reciprocity means that if you can make the other person feel indebted to you they are more likely to pay that debt with positive behavior. This is a powerful tactic used in sales and has saved large corporations from going bankrupt when used on a large scale.

- If the other party escalates their behavior by raising their voice, using profanity, indexing common places for weapons, begins looking around nervously, cutting you off from an exit route, suddenly goes quiet and stares "through" you, or constantly attempts to decrease distance and keep you directly in front of them, it's time to prepare for physical violence. Depending on the situation, if a combination of these factors are present the best plan is for you to initiate the physical confrontation.

Module 2 Conclusion

Interpersonal Communication Skills (IPCS) is an integral component of Control Tactics Training. Communication skills increase safety by defusing emotions and thereby reducing the likelihood of violence.

There are 5 techniques that officer's can use to build report and skillfully resolve a verbal altercation. They are *Listen*, *Empathize*, *Ask* questions, *Paraphrase* responses, and create a *Reciprocal* Relationship. As well there are some escalation phrases that should be avoided. They include making promises or threats, using phrases such as "calm down" or "relax" and using disrespectful verbal and non-verbal communication.

Depending on the situation verbal de-escalation may not be possible due to a subject's decisions and actions. While engaged in verbal communication officer's should be scanning for threat cues in the subject's verbal and body language. If physical force is Ethically and Legally warranted than officers should escalate to physical force.

> ## Module 3. Use of Force
>
> It is crucial that participants thoroughly understand what Canadian law is surrounding the Use Of Force. It is critical that each participant be able to understand the appropriate sections of the criminal code and have a working understanding of the underlying principles in the sections regulating use of force.
>
> This section is not intended to substitute legal studies but rather to be used as a refresher and to help participants understand the framework of how, when, and why force is applied to Canadian Citizens during altercations with Law Enforcement.

Chapter Testing Objectives

1. At the end of this session each participant will be able to:
2. Explain sections 25, 26, and 27 of the Canadian Criminal Code
3. Explain what is meant by "Totality of Circumstances"
4. Explain consequences of excessive force

Use of Force

The Canadian Criminal Code (CCC) contains guidelines for Peace Officers, Police, Public Officers, and Private Citizens for using force against another person in Canada.

Instead of trying to fit these laws and their underlying principles into a visual model, which would be limiting in its application, officers should instead thoroughly understand what the laws are and how to apply them and critically think in stressful circumstances. This is achieved by first understanding what the law says, then reviewing its application through case studies, then applying this understanding in theoretical table top studies, and then applying this understanding in physical practice.

Canadian Criminal Code

Section 25

25. (1) Every one who is required or authorized by law to do anything in the administration or enforcement of the law

(*a*) as a private person,
(*b*) as a peace officer or public officer,
(*c*) in aid of a peace officer or public officer, or
(*d*) by virtue of his office,

is, if he acts on reasonable grounds, justified in doing what he is required or authorized to do and in using as much force as is necessary for that purpose.

R.S., 1985, c. C-46, s. 25; 1994, c. 12, s. 1.

Discussion

Engage participants in class discussion and throughout the discussion combine questions and lecture to illustrate the following points;

- Private Persons and Peace officers may use force
- Force may be used in the enforcement of law
- Officers may use force to protect themselves OR someone else
- That force must meet the **Reasonable** Grounds Standard
- In the case of using force to protect life the officer must believe the assault was **Imminent**
- Officers are not required by law to pick the *best* use of force option. They are required to pick a *reasonable* option.
- The *best* use of force is always the reasonable option that results in the least harm to subject's, officers, the public, and the least property damage.
- An officer's number 1 priority when picking a use of force option should always be public safety, followed by officer safety, subject safety, and extent of property damage.

> Section 26
>
> Excessive force
>
> **26.** Every one who is authorized by law to use force is criminally responsible for any excess thereof according to the nature and quality of the act that constitutes the excess.
>
> R.S., c. C-34, s. 26.

Discussion

Engage participants in class discussion and throughout the discussion combine questions and lecture to illustrate the Totality of Circumstances to help participants understand the difference between Reasonable and Excessive Force;

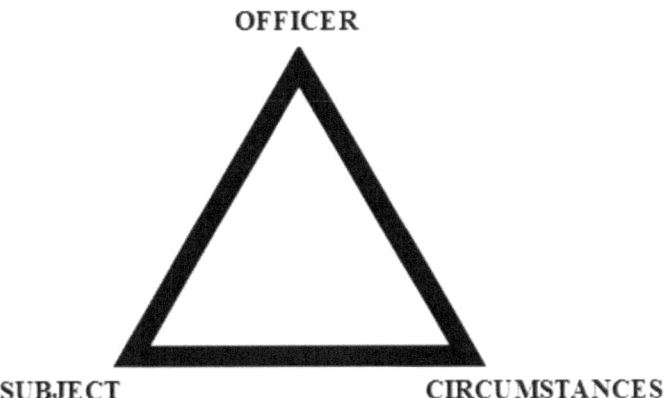

OFFICER

SUBJECT CIRCUMSTANCES

The graphic above illustrates that in order for officers to determine what a reasonable option and what an excessive option is they must take into account 3 factors. They are Officer Variables, Subject Variables, and Circumstantial Variables.

1. Officer Variables.

There are several variables that an officer(s) bring into the situation that will determine what force is reasonable for that situation. They include, but aren't limited to;

- Height, weight, build
- Fitness level
- Hydration and nutrition
- Exhaustion
- Skill set
- Confidence level
- Equipment
- Availability of backup
- Number of officers present at scene

2. Subject Variables.

There are several variables that a subject(s) bring into the situation that will determine what force is reasonable for that situation. These factors are always in relation to the Officer Factors. They include, but aren't limited to;

- Height, weight, build
- Observable fitness level indicators
- Observable skill set indicators
- Observable confidence level indicators
- Observable indicators of mental health concerns or intoxication
- Observable indicators or subject's willingness to co-operate with officers
- Weapons
- Number of subject's present at scene

3. Subject Variables.

There are several variables that circumstance(s) during a situation that will determine what force is reasonable for that situation. These factors are always in relation to the Officer and Subject Factors. They include, but aren't limited to;

- Original reason for officer and subject having contact with each other
- Seriousness of any offences being committed
- Environmental variables (light, weather, footing, environmental dangers, environmental weapons)
- Availability of escape for both officers and subject's
- Availability of Shielding, Cover, and Concealment
- Known history or intelligence surrounding the Subject or the situation
- Officers ability to maintain distance to the subject(s)

Totality of Circumstances

The term totality of circumstances therefore can be thought of as the relationship between the Officer(O), the Subject(S), and the Circumstances(C). This relationship can be visually represented as

This process must be completed very quickly and be ongoing. As a situation unfolds this relationship will continue to change. Research indicates that these changes can happen as quickly as $1:100^{th}$ of a second. This means that officers must continually be asking themselves what their reasonable force options during a situation or a confrontation.

Consequences of Excessive Force

Whether through negligence or on purpose officers who are found to have used excessive force during a situation or confrontation may be faced with the following repercussions;

- Termination of employment
- Criminal charges/conviction
- Civil liabilities from victims, families, or employers

> **Section 27**
>
> **Use of force to prevent commission of offence**
>
> **27.** Every one is justified in using as much force as is reasonably necessary
>
> (*a*) to prevent the commission of an offence
>
> >(i) for which, if it were committed, the person who committed it might be arrested without warrant, and
> >
> >(ii) that would be likely to cause immediate and serious injury to the person or property of anyone; or
>
> (*b*) to prevent anything being done that, on reasonable grounds, he believes would, if it were done, be an offence mentioned in paragraph (*a*).
>
> R.S., c. C-34, s. 27.

Discussion

Engage participants in class discussion and throughout the discussion combine questions and lecture to help them understand that they may use force to prevent Criminal Offences. Some examples to use are;

- A subject is about to break into a property but hasn't completed the offence yet
- A subject is about to vandalize a property but hasn't completed the offence yet
- A subject is about to assault someone but an officer isn't sure if it meets the Imminent requirement
- An officer believes a subject is going to flee lawful custody so applies mechanical restraints or an escort position

Module 3 Conclusion

During a control tactics or combat situation Officers are responsible for their decisions and actions. Officers are allowed to use force but the Canadian Criminal Code and Case law have defined what that force can be. Sections 25, 26, and 27 of the Canadian Criminal Code define an Officers force options as **Reasonable**, and cannot be **Excessive**.

To define which options in a tactical scenario are Reasonable and which are Excessive officers must take into account the Totality of Circumstances which is defined as the relationship and factors between the **Officer(s), the Subject(s), and the Circumstances** which brought them together. This relationship can be summarized as **O+S+C=Reasonable Force**.

If a court finds that officers used excessive force, that officer may find themselves subject to criminal conviction and penalty.

Module 4. Mechanical Restraint Application and Searching

One of the most basic, but most important, skills an officer can develop is their ability to place a detained or arrested subject into mechanical restraints. Although there are many different types of restraints with specific features and techniques for application, this module will cover a basic method for applying handcuffs to a co-operative subject who's standing up and a co-operative or resistant subject in the prone position.

As well once the subject is placed into handcuffs a search procedure will be demonstrated and performed by participants.

Chapter Testing Objectives

1. Perform the standing handcuff application technique.
2. Perform the prone handcuff application technique.
3. Perform a standing pat down search.

Understanding Handcuffs

Before learning how to handcuff someone you must first understand how handcuffs work.

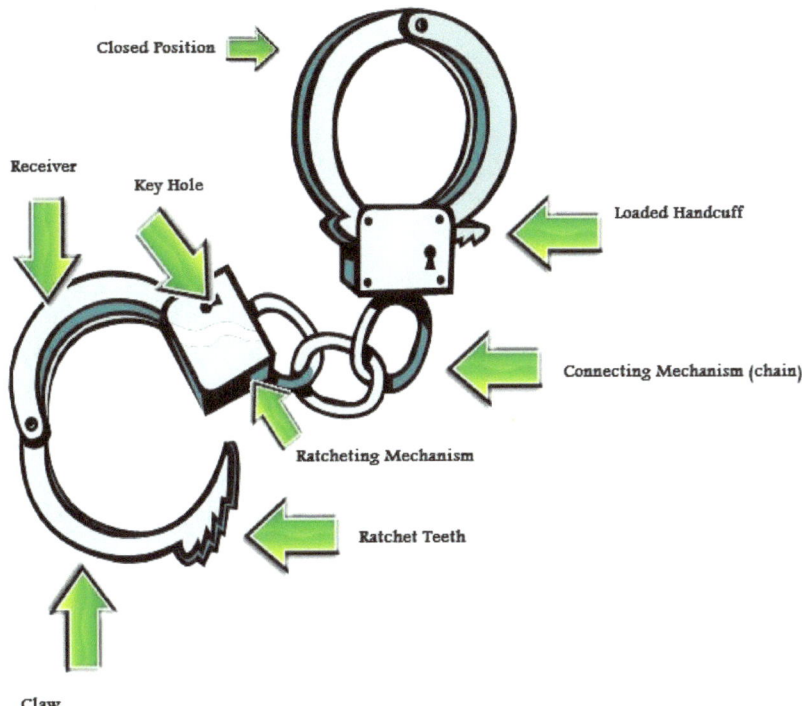

- Handcuffs basically work on a cycle where the Claw is pushed through the Receiver. It will depress the spring on the Ratcheting Mechanism and allow the Claw to cycle all the way around and through back into the Receiver.
- The spring loaded Ratcheting Mechanism won't allow the Claw to be pulled open (Closed Position).
- Once the Double Lock Mechanism is used the spring loaded Ratcheting Mechanism won't depress allowing the Claw to cycle (Double Locked Handcuff).
- By Loading the handcuff there is less friction during a cycle and the operation is smoother.

Technique #1. Standing Handcuff Application.

1. Gripping the Handcuffs

There are 2 methods for gripping the handcuffs. They are the Standard Grip and the Angle Grip. Generally speaking most officers use the standard grip. However for officers with large hands who find that their palm interferes with the claw cycling the angle grip might have to be used.

Standard Grip   Angle Grip

Either method can be used with standard chain handcuffs or hinged handcuffs. In the case of rigid handcuffs only the Standard Grip can be used.

2. Applying the Handcuffs

- To apply the handcuffs the officer first uses verbal communication skills to direct the subject into the I Position.

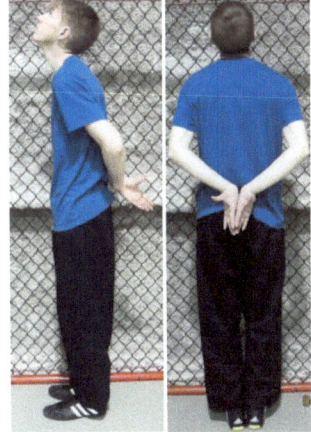

- Once the subject is in position and the officer has informed them to stay still, then the officer removes their handcuffs from their holder and establishes their grip.
- Next the officer moves to contact the subject gripping either both of the subject's hands or whichever hand mirrors the officers dominant hand (I.E. the one holding the handcuffs), and align the handcuff with the subject's wrist.

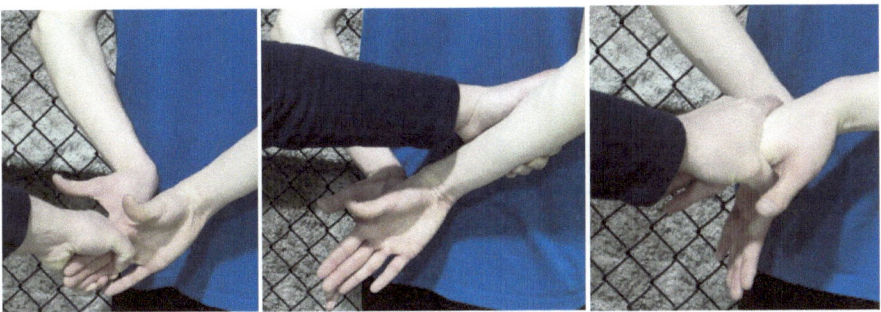

- Once grip is established push the handcuff onto the wrist
- If necessary re-establish a grip to the subject's free hand and manipulate as necessary to line up the handcuff
- Once grip and alignment are established push the second handcuff onto the wrist
- Fit check the handcuffs and double lock them

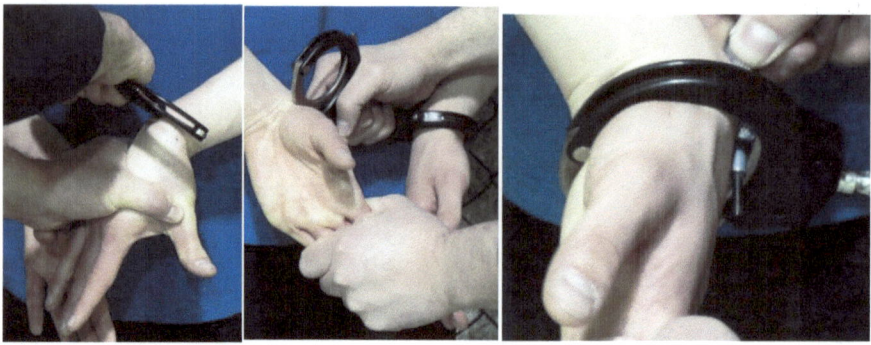

Technique #2. Prone Handcuff Application.

1. Establishing Prone Control

To establish prone control an officer uses a combination of anchoring the subject to the ground with body weight, controlling their head movement, blocking the subject's hands, and uses a joint lock combination to apply pain if needed.

Applying Prone Control

- Place 1 knee across the subject's' spine in between their shoulder blades. Be careful to avoid neck pressure.
- Lift the subject's arm off the ground and apply a combination Compression Wrist lock and Arm Bar with pressure towards the subject's head and down to the ground.
- Place the opposite knee on the ground. This method of posture prevents the subject from getting their hand to the ground, pockets, or front of their waistband should the arm lockout fail.
- Reach across the subject with the free hand and place it on the ground. This prevents the subject from accessing their pocket or front waistband.

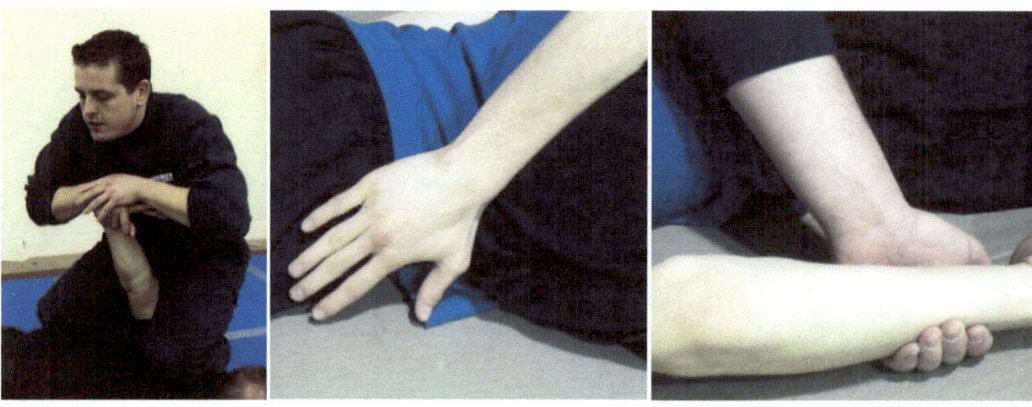

2. Applying the Handcuffs

- Once prone control is established then the officer accesses their handcuffs and establishes a **Standard Grip**.
- Next the officer aligns the handcuff secured in the bottom of their grip (I.E. between the pinky finger and palm) with the subject's wrist with their own palm up.

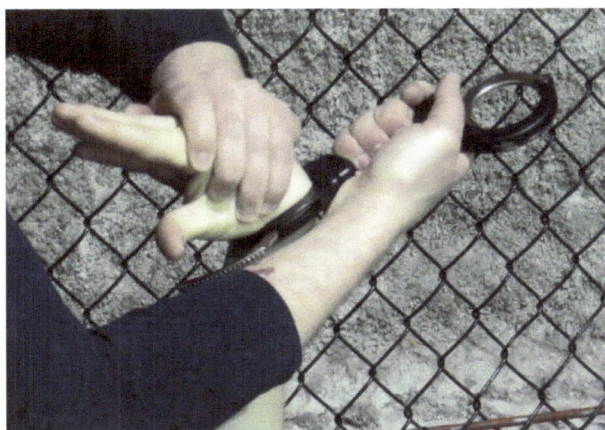

- Once grip and alignment are established push the handcuff onto the wrist
- Then the officer uses verbal commands or physical control to pull the subject's opposite (far) hand to the small of their back.
- Establish a grip to the subject's free hand and manipulate as necessary to line up the handcuff
- Once grip and alignment are established push the second handcuff onto the wrist

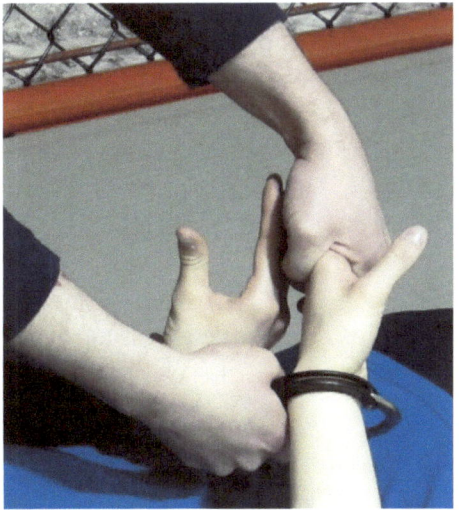

- Fit check the handcuffs and double lock them

Technique #3. Standard Field Search.

1. Pat Down

As discussed in Module 3, Officers have the lawful authority to perform a search after a Subject is arrested. Officer can remember the field search pattern with an acronym ALT-C. This acronym stands for;

- Ask – maintain verbal communication at all times with the subject asking questions about what weapons or objects of concern they might have on them. Maintain professionalism and do not make jokes about any items you're looking for. Gage the subject's responses for threat cues.
- Look- As always officers should be watching what they're doing and assessing any strange bulges or shapes in a subject's clothing or assessing any high risk areas during the search (I.E. waistbands, socks, boots, deep pockets).
- Touch- As officers search a light touch in each area is used to maximize safety and focus attention to that area. DO NOT run your hand over an area.
- Confirm – if something out of the ordinary is detected either by Asking, Looking, or Touching, the office must Confirm what it is by pressing it, slowly and gently squeezing the area or item, or removing items from the subject for visual inspection.
- Utilize the systematic approach quartering the subject's' body front and rear searching anything within reach without being off balance.
- Use the thumb lock and leg pressure technique to maintain control of subject.

Module 4 Conclusion

Handcuffing and searching are both basic skills but are very important to maximize officer safety. In the case of a standing handcuff application it's important for officers to demonstrate proficiency to deter the subject from resisting. It's also important to secure the handcuffs in as short a time frame as possible in an attempt to beat the subject's reaction time if they decide to resist after first contact.

During the prone technique officers are at a much higher risk of an altercation because they are sacrificing mobility and base for control. It is critically important to develop the arm lockout method to keep as much control as possible over the subject. Failure to do so may put officers at risk for a ground fight.

Searching not only helps ensure the arresting officers safety but the safety of any officer who takes custody of a subject and any members of the public or other detainees that the subject might come into contact with.

Instructor Notes

Standing Handcuffing

1. It is common for participants to struggle with gripping the handcuffs. Be sure to demonstrate the importance of not letting the bracelets move after grip is established. Participants with larger hands may struggle with the finger placement in the Angle Grip.
2. When applying the handcuffs participants will very often want to handcuff the subject's cross hand first with the bracelet secured by their own thumb and index finger. Be sure to demonstrate why that bracelet may need to be manipulated later and how much easier it is to secure the bracelet secured between the pinky finger and palm.
3. Participants will quit often lower their field of vision when establishing a grip on their handcuffs. Watch for this and demonstrate how to raise the handcuffs up into their vision to watch the subject while securing grip.
4. Participants will often manipulate their handcuffs while using verbal control to the subject. Help them develop good habits by not allowing them to have handcuffs in their hand while talking to the subject.
5. Participants may secure the handcuff high on a subject's arm or perpendicular to the shape of the wrist. Demonstrate the proper method and if they're struggling with application slow the speed of reps and help them manipulate the subject's wrist and handcuff.
6. Some subject's arms rest against their back. Demonstrate how to use a lumbar press and wrist pull to clear space for the handcuff to cycle.
7. Some subject's are too broad across the shoulders to secure with 1 pair of handcuffs. Demonstrate how to use 2 pair properly and open class discussion to include securing a handcuffed person to a c-spine board for medical emergencies.

Prone handcuffing

1. Watch for participants putting their knee/shin across a subject's neck and help them learn proper leg placement.
2. It is common for participants to rush through the prone handcuff procedure and make mistakes. The most common of these are not aligning the handcuff properly or letting the bracelet fall down the subject's forearm. Demonstrate and explain methods to solve this problem and ensure participants understand that they can slow down and take time to trouble shoot solutions to any problems that occur so long as they maintain control.

Searching

1. Participants will often rush the search and run their hand along areas. Ensure they understand the danger of this and that it can lead to serious injury and puncture wounds from needles.

> ## Module 5. Edged Weapon Defense
>
> Edged Weapons are a growing concern to officers. They are nearly impossible to regulate and can take the various forms, shapes and sizes. As well an assailant can cause serious injury and death with little training or skill.
>
> At the end of this session participants must be able to defend against an Ambush Edged Weapon attack

Chapter Testing Objectives

1. Demonstrate and understanding of the dangers of edged weapons.
2. Demonstrate the Block, Trap, Reap technique.

Understanding Edged Weapons

Before learning how to defeat an edged weapon attack participants must first be aware of the realities of these threats.

- Edged weapons damage on a cycle where the weapon is trusted out in either a stabbing motion or a slicing motion, pulled back, and repeated.
- Interrupting the cycle is critical to surviving an assault of this nature.
- Once the cycle is interrupted tactical superiority must be established through use of a takedown.
- Knives can damage tissue on the positive (thrusting) part of a cycle or the negative (pulling back) part of a cycle.
- Knives can cause harm and damage on many angles, do not malfunction, and do not run out of ammunition.
- Because of the close contact range of a knife attack it's very easy for the assailant to hit the target.
- Because of the speed of the cycles it's very difficult to interrupt them.
- Because of arm speed it's very difficult to grab a subject's hand or wrist during an assault.
- It's rare that people will die from a single knife wound. For this reason if struck with the knife officers must continue to take decisive action to protect themselves.
- The best strategy is to find cover, shielding, create space, or escape and engage with a firearm from distance.
- Because most attackers will use an ambush tactic however it's nearly impossible to access a firearm before the assailant can begin to injure the officer with the knife.
- Edged Weapon assaults are a lethal force threat

Technique #1. Intercepting the Cycle.

- When the subject attacks with the knife;
- Officer moves into the subject's power band and intercepts the attacking arm with 1 or both hands.

- The officer reaches over the subject elbow grabbing it in a full grip and tucking it against their body.

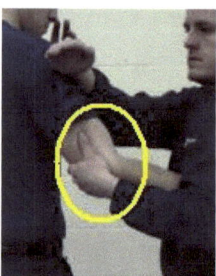

- Next the officer applies strikes to the subject's head and body.

This method can be used from any angle the knife travels along.

Technique #2. Leg Reap.

After an officer has intercepted and stopped a knife's cycle they should seek to take the subject down to the ground or if they believe their life is still in danger, and are equipped to do so, engage with contact fire with a sidearm.

Taking the subject down

- Drive past the subject while simultaneously lifting their head with a chin lift from either the hand or the elbow.

- The officer then brings their inside leg forward and behind the subject to swing it back and between the subject's legs.

- The Reap from the leg is from the hip and takes the foot in a **straight line** through the subject's' center effectively kicking out one leg. This motion combined with the force being applied to the subject's' jaw tilting their head back takes their balance and forces them to fall to the ground.

Technique #3. Follow up control.

Once the officer has control of the subject on the ground they must decide if they're going to continue to engage and attempt to control the subject or are they going to break away, get distance, and engage with other means or escape the situation.

- Dropping into a power squat position as the subject falls and turning into them the officer can maintain the subject's arm position.

- Depending on the nature of the attack control strategies will change. From this position either the Arm Bar Roll Over or the Wrist Twist Rollover is used to put the subject in a prone position and ½ Mount Control Handcuffing is used to secure the subject into mechanical restraints.

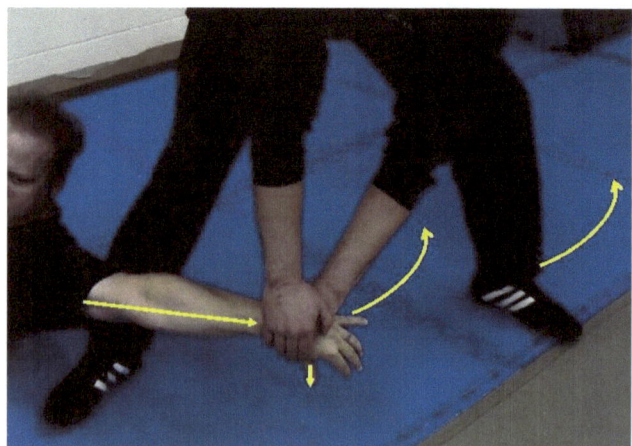
Arm bar rollover

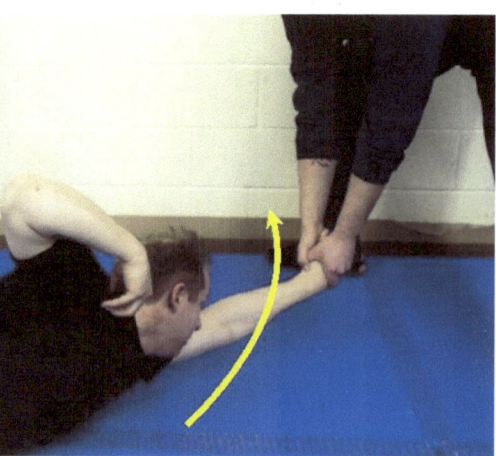
Wrist twist rollover

Module 5 Conclusion

An Edged Weapon assault is one of the most serious threats an officer could face in their career. It takes very little skill for the subject to be deadly with a knife but a high degree of skill for officers to protect themselves in contact range. Remember priority number 1, Don't Get Hit. While it's unlikely that a single wound will kill a person it is possible. A slash or puncture to the head, face, neck, or spine could be fatal.

Because of this distance, shielding, cover, and escape should be the primary options used if threatened by a knife. If however these aren't available it is imperative that the officer interrupts the attack from cycling and then takes the subject down to gain a positional advantage. From here the officer will have to choose to break contact with the subject or continue to attempt to control and arrest them.

Instructor Notes

Intercepting the Cycle

1. It is a common mistake either grab the assailant's forearm OR for the officer to use their forearm to attempt to hook the subject. Either one of these errors will allow for the subject to pull their arm free and continue attacking with that arm.
2. Some participants will want to move backwards. Demonstrate proper footwork for them to move forwards and intercept the subject's power band.
3. Demonstrate strikes to the subject's head and body and let participants practice this.

Leg Reap

1. The most common mistake is that officers will plant their leg and try to push subject's over it.
2. The second most common mistake is twisting or turning during this process.
3. Some participants will struggle with maintaining subject head control. Demonstrate both the hand and elbow press and pull down on the subject's elbow at the same time.

Follow up control

1. Participants will often rush lose balance when taking the subject down. Ensure to place emphasis on footwork during the demonstration and participant performance.

Module 6. Pressure Points and Facilitation Targets

The use of pressure points has been widely used and accepted in Law Enforcement for decades. Pressure Points, like any other technique, have a time and place to be attempted.

Facilitation Targets can help officers control subject's and situations at high levels of violence and can be worked into any other technique or skill.

Chapter Testing Objectives

1. Demonstrate an understanding of when to apply pressure points.
2. Demonstrate the Cranial Pressure Points to gain co-operation from a subject.
3. Demonstrate an understanding of when to apply facilitation targets.
4. Demonstrate the use of Facilitation Targets during counter-assault techniques.

Understanding Pressure Points

Before practicing the application of pressure points it's important to have a conceptual understanding of their application.

- Pressure Points are different then Facilitation Targets. Pressure points are used on a subject who is demonstrating a low level of resistance.
- There are two methods of applying pain to pressure points. They are Touch Pressure and Striking.
- There must be pressure-counter pressure. If there is no counter pressure the subject will simply pull away from the pain and the pressure point will not be effective.
- Punishment-reward principle. Pain is caused through the pressure points in various methods to counter resistance. Once the subject complies with the officers commands the pressure must be alleviated or else the subject's behavior and level of resistance is likely to escalate to the level where pressure points are no longer effective.
- Not everyone is as sensitive to these pressure points. For this reason if an officer is attempting to use a pressure point to gain control of a subject and it's not working they should switch tactics after 3 seconds of the pressure point being ineffective.

Technique #1.
Cranial Pressure Points.

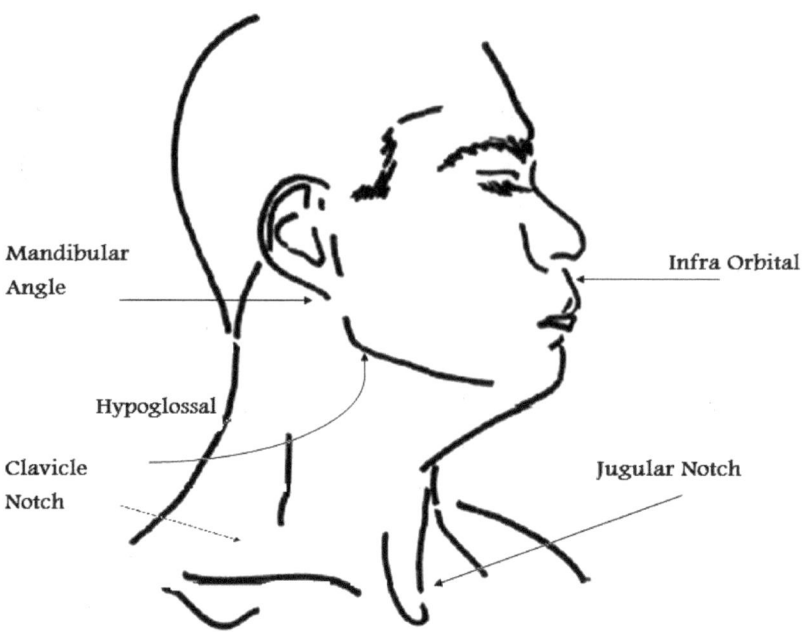

- To use the **Mandibular Angle** pressure point officers first stabilize the subject's head as mentioned above. The point itself is located behind the base of the ear lobe between the mastoid and the mandible. Once having located the area officers make a fist with the tip of their thumb protruding slightly past the knuckles. Pressure is applied in and slightly up towards the tip of the nose. Pressure is applied until the subject becomes compliant.
- To use the **Infra Orbital** pressure point officers must first stabilize the subject's head as mentioned above. The point of contact is located at the base of the nose where the septum meets the skull above the upper lip. Pressure is applied at a 45-degree angle towards the top of the head using the side of the middle knuckle in the index finger. Pressure is applied until the subject becomes compliant.
- The **Hypoglossal** pressure point is located approximately 1 inch forward of the "R" angle of the mandible and 1 inch under the jaw in the notch of the jaw bone. The head is stabilized and pressure is directed toward the top of the center of the head using the tip of the thumb supported by the first and second fingers. Pressure is applied until the subject becomes compliant.
- The **Jugular Notch** is primarily used to push a subject down or back. From in front of the subject the officer uses the index and middle finger in a hook shape to dig inside the hollow point in the notch at the base of the neck, just above the sternum. The officer drives their fingers in and down to force the subject backwards and to the ground.
- **Clavicle Notch** is located directly behind the clavicle approximately half way between the sternum and shoulder. The officer again uses the middle and index finger and drives their finger tips into the hollow behind the bone in and down at a 45 degree angle to force the subject to the ground.

Pressure Points in the Arm

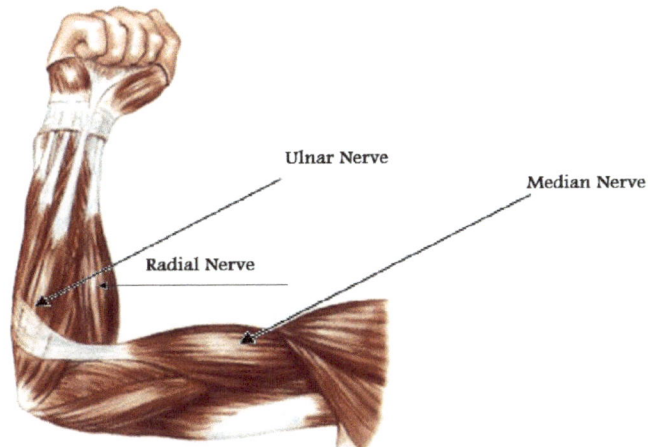

- The **Radial Nerve** is located on top of the forearm approximately 2 inches below the elbow. The officer should strike this area towards the center of the arm to cause numbness and pain.
- The **Ulnar Nerve** is located in the inside of the forearm just above the base of the palm in the wrist. This area is primarily used in impact weapon blocking and striking here can cause numbness and pain.
- The **Median Nerve** is located in the bicep. The officer should strike into the belly of the bicep to cause numbness and pain.

Pressure Points in the Leg

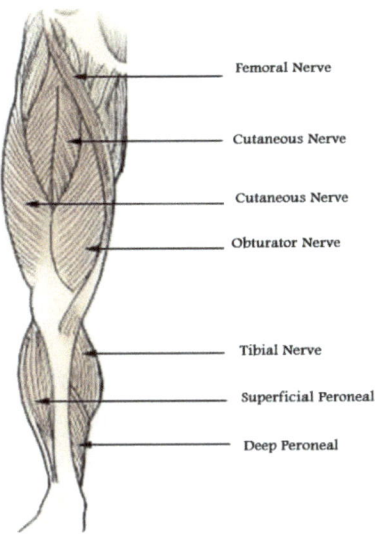

- There are 7 facilitation targets in the leg.
- The **Tibial Nerve** starts just above the outside of the thigh and runs down the back of the leg into the calf. Strikes should be delivered just at the top of the calf below the knee. This area is primarily struck from behind to cause a numbness, pain, and loss of balance.
- The **Superficial Peroneal Nerve** is located at the base of the shin just above the instep. Strikes to this area are designed to cause pain and numbness as well as loss of balance.
- The **Femoral**, **Cutaneous**, and **Obturator Nerves** are all located in the muscle of the upper thigh. This is a very sensitive area and striking here can cause pain, numbness, and loss of balance.

Technique #2. Facilitation Targets.

Facilitation targets are struck at higher levels of resistance, assault, or deadly force assaults.

- As mentioned previously there is a big difference between Facilitation Targets and pressure points. A pressure point is a nerve motor point that is over stimulated to cause a sensation of pain in the brain. Facilitation Targets are not necessarily nerve motor points but probably small bones that are easily manipulated or soft sensitive tissue that is easily damaged. Where a focused individual might be able to withstand pressure point pain the application of a pain sensitive area will likely cause damage to that area and render the use of that body part impossible. Following are a few examples of Facilitation strikes and how they can be applied. Instructors are encouraged to build upon this list and to encourage participants to think of new applications when involved in a dynamic situation. Participants are to be reminded however that they are responsible for any technique used and must be able to justify and articulate the reasons for relying on Facilitation strikes.
- Eyes. The eyes are a very sensitive area that are easy to damage. An officer can cause a distraction by simply flicking something towards the eyes or can cause blindness by clawing and striking them. For this reason the eyes can be used as a PSA for many different levels of resistance. Participants are to be reminded that when using any technique that involves the eyes there is a risk of permanent injury to the subject and they have to be able to articulate why they were legally justified in attacking this sensitive area.
- Fingers and Toes. The fingers and toes are made up of several small bones and connective tissue. For this reason they are very susceptible to injury and pain. An officer may use a finger lock to acquire pain compliance or in a highly combative situation might break the fingers to render a subject's weapon delivery hand useless. Toes may be crushed under extraordinary circumstances to limit the mobility of a subject.
- Mouth. The mouth is another area of the body that is very easily damaged. Fishhooks and tearing of the lips and gums are often over looked techniques of opportunity in highly dynamic and confrontational situations.
- Groin. Many control tactics programs don't advocate strikes to the groin for liability purposes. This area is very sensitive and easily damaged. Under life or death circumstances however a strong strike to the groin may render a subject immobile.
- Throat. Again the throat is a very sensitive area that might cause death or permanent injury. For this reason strikes to the throat should only be used as a last ditch resort in deadly force

confrontations where the officer has no other choice and must stop a subject's actions immediately and where lethal force is justified.
- Hair. The hair is a great tool because the likelihood of permanent injury is very low. Violently pulling on a subject's hair will cause great pain and will pull the head out from over the center of gravity causing a Balance Displacement.
- Ears. Ears are another very sensitive target area. They can be struck, grabbed and pulled, or torn off depending of the dynamics of the confrontation.

Module 6 Conclusion

An understanding of Pressure Points can assist officers when dealing with low levels of resistance from subject's. Offices should remember however that there is a percentage of the population resistant or immune to pain from pressure points and that during a high level of resistance, generally speaking in the form of an assault, pressure points should not be attempted.

Having an understanding of Facilitation Targets can help officers to end a violent altercation quickly. The longer a violent altercation lasts the higher the likelihood of harm to the public, the officer, and the subject. Different facilitation targets will be legally and ethically justifiable depending on the totality of circumstances.

Instructor Notes

Pressure Points

1. The number one most common participant mistake is to not apply counter pressure.
2. Some participants will be very close to locating a pressure point but still having difficulty finding it. Demonstrate the oscillation method to pinpoint the location.
3. Some participants will be too timid to apply pressure to their training partner. Demonstrate safe methods for practice to help them feel comfortable.

Facilitation Targets

1. Once the Facilitation Targets module has been delivered encourage them to use touch application throughout the rest of their training practice.

> ## Module 7. Control Holds
>
> Control holds are excellent techniques for use on a co-operative subject or subject's exhibiting low levels of resistance.
>
> Control holds basically work by "locking" a joint to control or manipulate the subject skeleton. Quit often it's the pain from the lock or the fear of breaking their own joint that will control the subject. For this reason control holds do not work well on high levels of resistant behavior or assaultive behavior because the subject will either use strength to force their way out of the lock or risk the injury and keep moving.

Chapter Testing Objectives

1. Demonstrate an understanding of when to attempt a Control Hold.
2. Demonstrate the Escort Position.
3. Demonstrate the Front Compression Wristlock.
4. Demonstrate the Rear Compression Wristlock.
5. Demonstrate the Straight Arm Bar Takedown.

Understanding Control Holds

Before practicing the application of Control Holds it's important to have a conceptual understanding of their application.

- There are 2 types of control holds. The first controls a subject through **pain and fear**. Putting pressure into joints past a normal range of motion causes discomfort which encourages the subject to cooperate with the officer. Once cooperation is obtained pressure is eased off as to not cause injury to the subject or undue suffering.
- The second type of joint manipulation is used to take a subject off balance by **using the joint and limb as leverage** and causes subject's to fall to the ground. This type of joint manipulation locks joints into place at the end of their range of motion and creates leverage to any one of the five areas of the body that manipulates balance.

Technique #1. The Escort Position

- Officers may use the escort position to escort a cooperative or a resisting subject. In the case of a non-cooperative subject officers may choose to use the escort position to determine if the subject will become physically resistant or not.
- To apply the escort position officers approach the subject in an athletic posture with their hands up in preparation of the subject suddenly becoming assaultive.
- First contact is made by the officer putting both hands on the subject's' upper arm.

- From this position both hands slide down the subject's arm. The hand inside the subject's arm stops just above the subject's elbow. The outside hand is slid down to the subject's' wrist. The officer then uses a c-clamp hold on the subject's' wrist to gain control.
- From here the subject's arm is pulled into the officers' body. The subject's arm should touch the officer.
- The officer holds the subject's hand on his hip opposite from the subject.

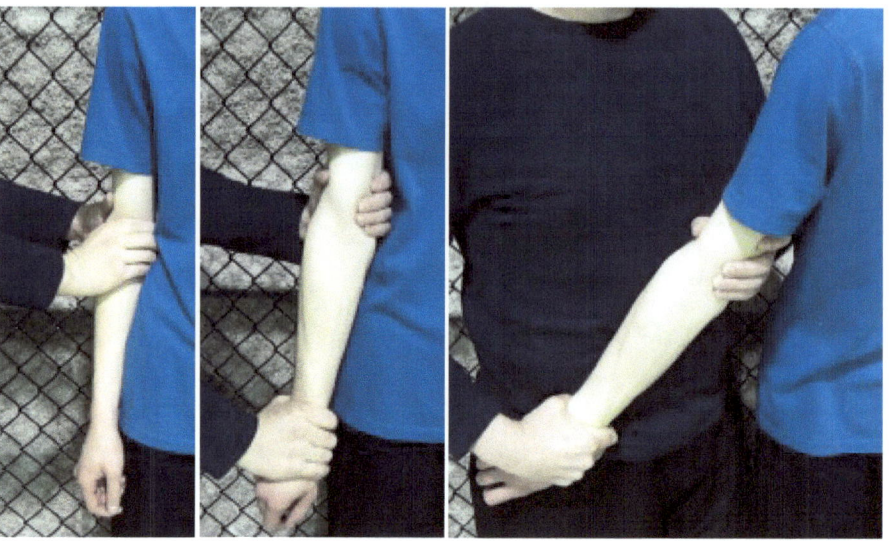

Technique #2. Front Compression Wristlock.

- The Front Compression Wristlock is used when a subject attempts curl their arm and bringing their hand tight to their chest.
- When the officer feels this resistance they are not to attempt to hold the arm in place against their body, but rather let the subject curl their arm.
- The officer delivers a knee strike to the mid thigh of the subject.
- The officer then uses the hand on the subject's wrist to push the subject's elbow and arm back against the officers rib cage. The hand that was on the subject's bicep shoots through the opening between the subject's rib cage and arm a grasps the back of the subject's hand.
- The officer delivers pressure on the back of the subject's wrist causing a "goose neck" and puts pressure on the index knuckle of the subject using their index finger.
- If required the officer can elevate the wrist of the subject to cause Pain Compliance.
- From the Front Compression Wristlock officers can handcuff the subject without losing control. To start this process the officer turns the subject's wrist so that their fingers point in towards their chest. The officer maintains control of the subject's wrist with their hand that is between the subject's arm and ribs. The officer accesses their handcuffs with their other hand and applies the top bracelet to the subject's bent wrist. The officer then rotates the subject's wrist back to the control position and rotates their hand around the base of the bracelet so that there palm is facing forwards.

- To finish the handcuffing process the officer steps back and brings the subject's arm behind them applying a steel wristlock. The officer then directs the subject to put their other hand behind their back and uses the inverted handshake to apply the second handcuff.

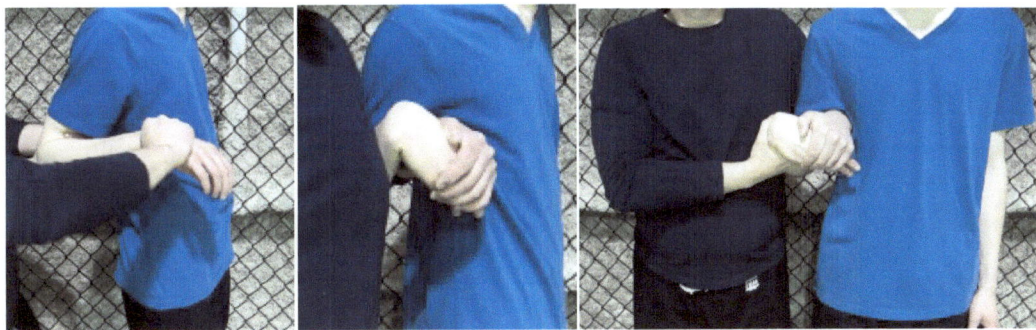

Technique #3. Rear Compression Wristlock.

- The Rear Compression Wrist Lock is used to establish control from either the Escort Position, the Front Compression Wristlock, or from the handcuffed position.
- From the Escort Position or the Front Compression Wristlock the officer simply drives the arm behind the subject's back by using their body and shoulder rotation. The forearm should be parallel to the ground.
- The officer then slides the hand furthest from the subject onto the back of the subject's hand and applies pressure in a "goose neck".
- From the handcuffed position the officer starts by facing the subject's side at 90 degrees.
- The officer then slides their arm closest to the subject's front between the subject's bicep and back.
- From this position the officer applies pressure on the back of the subject's index knuckle for pain compliance and escorts the subject backwards to the intended destination.

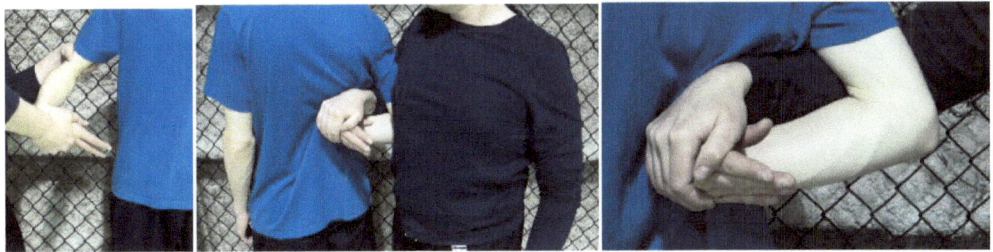

Technique #4. Straight Arm Bar Takedown.

- The Straight Arm Bar Takedown is an example of joint manipulation to use a limb as a lever to affect to take a subject off balance.

- The Straight Arm Bar Takedown is initiated when a subject straightens their arm from the Escort Position. The subject will lock out their elbow and often attempt to pull away from the officer.
- When the officer feels this lockout resistance they respond by using the Straight Arm Bar Takedown.
- To begin the technique the officer first ensures that the subject is tight to their body and that the subject's' hand is on the officers opposite hip.
- Next the officer uses a knee strike to the subject's mid thigh.
- The officer then places the flat part of their wrist that's providing support at the subject's elbow up to the outside of the subject's shoulder. Using a scooping motion the officer rolls their wrist down to the elbow and digs the ulnar notch of their wrist into the tricep of the subject while simultaneously pulling the subject closer to them.

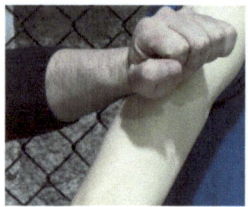 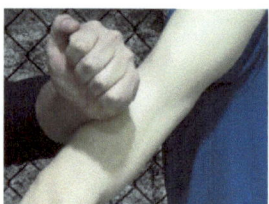 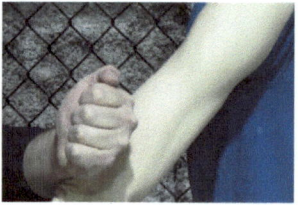 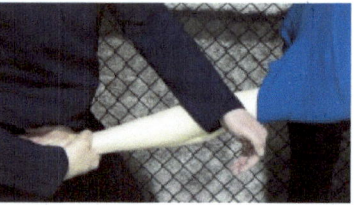

- The officer provides pressure on the top of the subject's elbow using a pulling motion at the elbow using the boney protrusion on the back of their wrist. This causes the subject to bend forwards at the waist causing them to be off balance.
- To finish the technique the officer slides their outside foot straight back and provide straight pressure to the ground.
- From this position the officer can either tactically disengage or control the subject using Prone Control Arm Lockout and restrain them using the Prone Handcuffing Technique.

Module 7 Conclusion

An understanding of Control Holds can allow officers to establish control or a takedown when dealing with low levels of resistance from subject's. Offices should remember however that there is a percentage of the population who will escalate their behavior from such attempts and defeat the control hold either with sheer strength or accepting the pain and fear and move through the attempted joint lock.

Another risk for officers is that once a control hold is attempted they're within the reactionary gap and generally very close range to the subject. It is therefore critical that before attempting control holds the office has an understanding of how to abandon the technique and link to another option which either continues control attempts at close range or moves the officer back out to a farther range allowing them different options.

Instructor Notes

Escort Position

1. The number one most common participant mistake is not keeping their hands up, making contact with the upper arm, and sliding down into position. Particularly after they've completed a number of repetitions laziness can set in and they'll start land marking the elbow and wrist for the grab. Be sure to illustrate how easy it is for a subject to create power and range of motion at the wrist but difficult to do the same at the upper arm.

Front Compression Wristlock

1. Participants may struggle with pulling the hand back and tucking under the armpit to create counter pressure. The most common reason for this is because they'll reach for the hand before tucking the subject's elbow and use their chest for counter pressure. If this happens illustrate how a subject can invert their elbow to escape the pressure and possibly strike the officer in the face at the same time. If necessary slow the participant down by having them demonstrate the technique and talking their way through it or following an instructors count.

Rear Compression Wristlock

1. Some participants will struggle with changing their hand position to ensure pressure is placed on the subject's knuckles. Demonstrate the different methods to change the hand to get to the right position.

Straight Armbar Takedown

1. Participants' will may not understand the timing between the step-pull-and scoop motions.
2. Participants may simply attempt to use strength to drag the subject down to the ground.
3. Participants may put themselves off balance by using their core and back to push on the subject's arm instead of the legs to pull into a squat position.

> **Module 8. Oleoresin Capsicum Spray**
>
> **Oleoresin Capsicum (OC) Spray is a Less Lethal force option for some agencies. It is not legal for non-Peace Officers to use however and therefore is not an option for security agencies.**
>
> **OC Spray combines natural ingredients which have a demonstrated effect at causing pain and swelling in the eyes and in general the goal of using it is to cause the subject's eyes to clamp shut thereby making them unable to see and focus their resistant or assaultive behavior.**

Chapter Testing Objectives

1. Demonstrate an understanding of how and why OC Spray works.
2. Demonstrate an understanding of the limitations of OC Spray.
3. Demonstrate different methods for engaging a subject with OC Spray.

Understanding OC Spray

Before practicing how to engage a subject with OC Spray, it's important to have a conceptual understanding of its application, effects, and limitations.

OC Spray is available in "Patrol" models as well as grenades, cell busters, and crowd control models that fog a wide area. Civilian Products are available to control animals. These are very dangerous because they aren't regulated the same as devices for use on people and may contain very dangerous chemicals. OC Spray for use on humans is classed as a prohibited weapon in Canada. OC Spray is manufactured by extracting Capsicum from peppers and mixing it with a carrier agent and a propellant.

There are some advantages to using OC Spray. Officers can eengage a subject at a distance and there is no risk of permanent injury to officer or the subject. It's easy to use and unaffected by external temperatures.

There some disadvantages however. It is adversely affected by wind and rain and the subject may avoid direct spray. The subject might also have eye covering (i.e. prescription glasses) and it may not take effect at all. There is a risk of user contamination in close quarters and some subject's may respond in an adverse manner and become more aggressive. Also the effects on dogs is inconclusive. OC Spray also should never be deployed within 1 meter of a subject's eyes except in extreme cases where no other option is available. Spraying a subject within 1 meter may cause **Ballistic Needling** where molecules have enough mass and velocity to become embedded in the tissue of the eye and cause injury.

Officers should primarily think of OC Spray as a distractionary device because its effects vary greatly from person to person. For this reason, just like with any other distractionary device, once deployed the officer(s) must be prepared for immediate follow up with physical control methods.

There are several different manufacturers and different methods of measuring the effectiveness of each product and different products are available. Regardless of which product an officer or agency is using there should be a maintenance protocol in place. Always differ to the manufacturers recommendations. Generally speaking it's recommended that product be replaced after 4 years because the internal components and valves might break down. Most agencies also require their officers to test with ¼ second burst (outdoors, downwind) monthly and inspect the canister regularly for damage.

OC Spray is Non – Flammable and safe to use in conjunction with a Conducted Energy Weapon or on a subject who is smoking. Effective Range differs according to model and manufacturers but is generally used no closer than 1 meter and begins to lose effectiveness after 9 meters (patrol models).

There are 2 methods for measuring the "hotness" of the product. They are Scoville Heat Units which are very subjective and Major Capsaicinoids which measures the amount of Capsaicin in the product.

When used on a subject, OC Spray affects 3 major physiological areas. They are the Respiratory System, the Eyes, and the Skin.

Respiratory System: OC Spray causes inflammation of mucus membranes and pronounced mucus secretion which can lead to coughing and shortness of breath.

Eyes: Visual impairment is the primary goal of using OC Spray. Capsicum absorbs water molecules which dries out the eyes causing a painful burning sensation and involuntary eye closure. It can also cause profound tearing and inflammation and redness.

Skin: Subject's can experience inflammation, intense burning, and redness.

As well as the physiological affects there are some **Psychological Effects.** These are **Fear, Panic, Thought process interruption, and Goal re-orientation.**

When an officer is deciding if OC Spray is a reasonable force option there are some observable factors to consider regarding the subject. Even if OC Spray is reasonable for the situation under normal circumstances these factors may lead an officer to change tactics and use a different option. They are the presents of **alcohol intoxication or drug influence, physical exertion, obesity, or any observable medical conditions.** When using OC Spray on subject's with any of these factors it may lead to an adverse affect where the subject becomes more violent or it may also cause a serious medical emergency because the subject can't breathe.

A cut-away diagram of a typical patrol model canister of OC Spray.

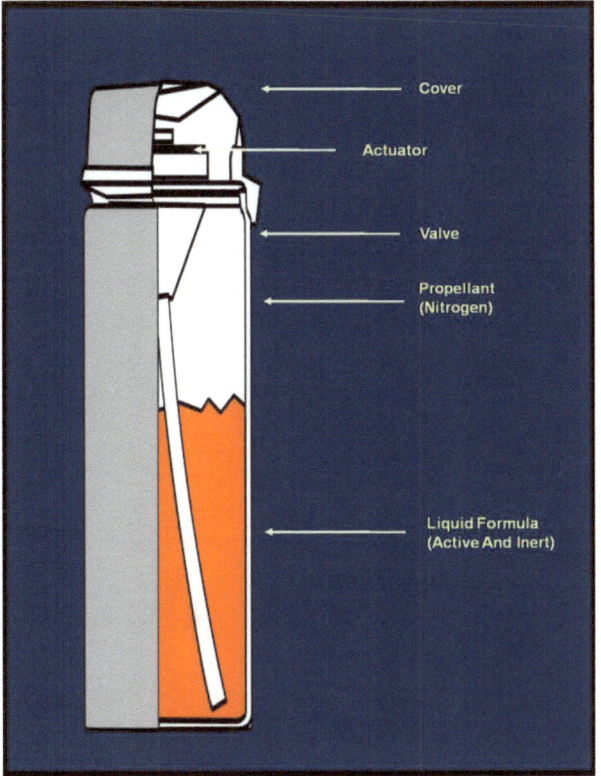

Decontamination

After someone is contaminated with OC Spray it becomes the officers responsibility to give that person reasonable care. Also it may be that an innocent member of the public or another officer has become contaminated. For these reasons it is important that any officer equipped with and authorized to use OC Spray be familiar with the decontamination process.

- **Verbal reassurance.** Reassure the contaminated person that the effects are temporary and that they'll be OK.

- **Rinse with clean water.** Because OC Spray absorbs water molecules the burning and pain usually won't subside until after the OC can't absorb anymore water. By exposing the contaminated area to fresh cool water it relieves the burning sensation and saturates the OC with more water than it can absorb.

- **Exposure to fresh, cool air.** In situations where water isn't available exposure to fresh, cool, moving air will also help relieve the burning and pain and dry out the OC Spray where it can be flaked off the contaminated person.

- **Remove contact lenses.** Officers should have anyone contaminated remove their contact lenses so that product doesn't get trapped between the lense and the tissue of the eye.

- **Remove contaminated clothing.** When possible remove contaminated clothing and replace it with clean clothing.

- **Do not apply salves, lotions, or creams.** Salves and creams can trap the OC on the skin and prevent air or water from getting to it which will prolong the discomfort from the OC Spray.

- **Seek medical attention if required.** Research suggests that most people begin to recover from the effects of OC Spray within 1 hour. If there is no change in a person's condition within this time seek medical attention. Also if the person begins to show signs of respiratory complications or allergic reaction seek medical attention immediately.

Using OC Spray

Technique #1. Basic technique

- The basic technique is used on subject who are greater than 1 meter distance from the OC Canister when the officer has their arm extended.
- The officer removes the OC Canister from its holster and extends their arm directly at the subject's' eyes.
- Using the thumb the officer lifts the safety cap and depresses down on the actuator.
- Using the stream of OC Spray as an indicator the officer makes small adjustments until they're sure they've contaminated the eyes.
- The officer puts the canister back into its holster or into a pocket and engages in follow up physical control techniques.

Technique #2. Close Quarter Technique

- The close quarter technique is for use when subject's are within 1 meter from the OC Canister when the officer has their arm extended.
- The officer uses 1 arm to drive the subject back or hold them at an extended arms distance while simultaneously removes the OC Canister from its holster with the other hand.
- The officer pulls their arm holding the OC Canister back as far as they can and aims directly at the subject's' eyes.
- Using the thumb the officer lifts the safety cap and depresses down on the actuator.
- Using the stream of OC Spray as an indicator the officer makes small adjustments until they're sure they've contaminated the eyes.
- The officer puts the canister back into its holster or into a pocket and engages in follow up physical control techniques.

Technique #3. Hand Contamination Technique

- The hand contamination technique is for use when subject's are within 1 meter from the OC Canister when the officer cannot create distance or doesn't have enough time to access the OC Spray out of its holster.
- In this case the officer leaves the OC in its holster and simply lifts the safety cover and depresses the actuator with the palm of their hand in front of the nozzle.
- This will spray product into the officers hand.
- The officer then takes their hand and uses touch contact to contaminate the subject's eyes with the OC Spray.

Module 8 Conclusion

The effectiveness of OC Spray is never guaranteed. Subject's vary a great deal in terms of how they react when contaminated. OC Spray does offer some advantages to the officer however. Generally speaking it allows the officer to engage from a safer distance and causes blindness, pain, fear, and panic in subject's giving officer a distinct advantage when they close the distance to use physical control techniques.

OC Spray should never be used as the primary option in a lethal force situation. Officers must also remember there are several things to take into account before using OC Spray such as the presence of the public, wind conditions, availability of medical treatment or decontamination stations, and any observable health risks posed by the subject.

Instructor Notes

1. Instructors are encouraged to become familiar with many different types of products and be able to educate officers on each. Some products will have different features such as being able to deploy spray while inverted.
2. Be sure to have plenty of inert spray on hand to allow participants the opportunity to work OC Spray techniques into their other skills and become proficient and comfortable using OC Spray.

> **Module 9. Baton Use**
>
> **Batons are impact weapons that can be lawfully carried by Peace Officers and in some areas security personnel who've successfully attended a recognized training program.**
>
> **Although using baton seems easy at first it can actually be challenging to effectively stop a subject's assaultive behavior with one. During stressful encounters officers often forget how to strike effectively and even though they deliver several blows it doesn't stop a subject. When using a baton the chance of injury to the subject increases exponentially. For these reasons it is imperative that officers are highly proficient using this force option.**

Chapter Testing Objectives

1. Demonstrate an understanding of the target areas of a subject.
2. Demonstrate the different strikes for engaging a subject with a baton.

Understanding the Baton.

Before practicing how to engage a subject with an impact weapon, it's important to have a conceptual understanding of its application, effects, and limitations.

Most agencies lawfully entitled to carry a Baton use an Expandable Model. These batons collapse into the closed mode for carrying and open telescopically to full length. The baton is primarily used in the open mode. In case of tight quarters or emergency time constraints the baton can be used in closed mode.

A baton is used when empty hand methods of controlling an assaultive subject have failed, or when the officer believes they will fail. In this application major muscle groups are struck and include the thighs and forearms. If striking the forearms and thighs fails to stop a subject and they are continuing their assaultive behavior than striking major joints may be necessary. In this case knees and elbows are the primary options.

In the case of a deadly force assault, and the officer has no other means to protect themselves, the baton may be used. In this case the officer would target the head, spine, hands, and groin.

Using the Baton

Technique #1. Opening and Closing a Friction Lock Expandable Baton

- Depending on the manufacturer there may be different methods of opening and closing a friction lock expandable baton

- The basic method will work with the majority of products and the in the majority of circumstances.
- The officer begins by removing their closed baton from its scabbard with their dominant hand.
- They raise the baton beside them so it's tip up and then violently drop their body weight down slightly from the knees and whip and the baton close to their body until it points tip down. This method should overcome the friction holding the baton closed and snap the sections of baton in place in the open mode.

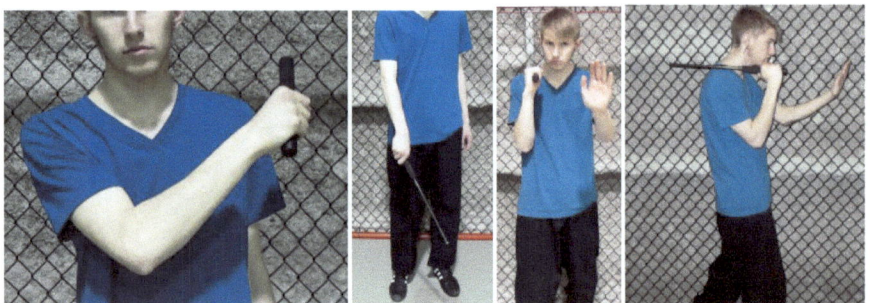

- From here the officer adopts the Open Position by bringing the baton up to their dominant shoulder and resting it on top of the shoulder with the butt cap pointing at their intended target.
- Depending on the circumstances the officer may adopt the Closed Position by crossing their arm across their body and resting the baton over their support arm bicep and shoulder.
- To close the baton the officer begins by inverting it and dropping it tip down onto a hard surface. This process may have to be repeated until the friction where the sections lock is overcome and the baton will collapse back to the closed mode.

Technique #2. Forehand Strike

- The Forehand Strike is the most powerful strike and officer can use and is the primary reason for using a baton.

- The Forehand Strike is typically delivered to the thigh of a subject in the hopes of causing a muscle cramp thereby forcing the subject to stop their assaultive behavior.
- From the Open Position the officer pushes off the ball of their dominant foot to rotate their hips and shoulders and swings the baton parallel to the ground into the intended target.
- The officer's grip should be palm up and hand parallel to the ground.
- The officer pushes the tip of the baton into the target before returning to the Open Position.

Technique #3. Backhand Strike

- The Backhand Strike is not as powerful as the Forehand strike and is delivered from the Closed Position.
- From the Closed Position the officer pushes off the ball of their support foot to rotate their hips and shoulders and swings the baton parallel to the ground into the intended target.
- The strike is delivered into the thigh of a subject in the hopes of causing a muscle cramp thereby forcing the subject to stop their assaultive behavior.
- The officer's grip should be palm down and hand parallel to the ground.
- The officer pushes the tip of the baton into the target before returning to the Closed Position.

Technique #4. Forehand and Backhand Blocking Strikes

- The Forehand and Backhand Blocking Strikes aren't as powerful as the Forehand and Backhand strike and are primarily delivered to a subject's forearms as the subject attacks with punches or in Deadly Force situations possibly an edged weapon attack.
- When delivering the Forehand and Backhand Blocking Strikes the strike is delivered in a slashing type motion.
- From the Open or Closed Position the officer pushes off the ball of their foot to rotate their hips and shoulders and swings the baton in an X like pattern from high to low into the intended target.

Technique #5. Closed Mode Butt Strike

- The Closed Mode Butt Strike can be used in close quarters or in instances where the officer didn't have time to open the baton.
- To deliver a Closed Mode Butt Strike the officer places their thumb over the tip of a Closed Baton and pushes off the ball of their foot to rotate their hips and shoulders and swings the baton in an X like pattern from high to low into the intended target.

Module 9 Conclusion

The effectiveness of striking a subject with a baton is never guaranteed. Subject's vary a great deal in terms of how they react when struck. An impact weapon does offer some advantages to the officer however. Generally speaking it allows the officer to engage from a safer distance and causes pain, fear, muscle cramping, and panic in subject's giving officer a distinct advantage when they close the distance to use physical control techniques.

Impact Weapons should never be used as the primary option in a lethal force situation. Officers must also remember there are several things to take into account before using a baton such as the availability of medical treatment, any observable health risks posed by the subject, and if the officer has the time to access their baton and the space to use it.

Instructor Notes

1. Instructors are encouraged to become familiar with many different types of products and be able to educate officers on each. Some products will have different features such as being able to deploy by being pulled open from the tip or use auto-locks instead of friction locks.
2. Be sure to have training batons, striking shields, and live batons before starting class.

Technique #1. Opening and Closing a Friction Lock Expandable Baton

1. Some officers will attempt to flick the baton from closed to open with wrist movement only and won't effectively use body mechanics. Even if this does open the baton it likely won't create a good friction lock and the baton may close during an altercation.

2. Some officers will "float" the baton in the Open or Closed Position. They should make sure the baton touches them to build in a tactile reference to where their baton is and aid in retention of the baton.
3. When closing some officers won't use direct downwards impact. This can bend and wreck a baton.

Technique #2. Forehand Strike

1. The most common mistake is for participants to "hack" into the target on a 45 degree angle instead of a 90 degree angle.
2. The second most common mistake is for people to strike without ensuring their palm is up. This can cause an inadvertent disarm by prying the baton from the officers grip on impact. Ensuring proper hand position helps make sure that opposite pressure travelling down the baton and into the hand is absorbed into the strongest part of the grip and palm of the hand.
3. The third most common mistake is for officers to start pulling the baton back to a ready position before all of the force from the strike goes into the target. Help officers to push the tip of the baton into the target to begin the cycle back to a ready position instead of simply pulling their hand back.
4. Watch for use of body mechanics, particularly foot, hip, and shoulder rotation.
5. Help participants aim with the butt of the baton before striking. This helps keep the path the tip of the baton travels along short which makes it harder for subject's to counter.

Technique #3. Backhand Strike

1. The most common mistake is for participants to "hack" into the target on a 45 degree angle instead of a 90 degree angle.
2. The second most common mistake is for people to strike without ensuring their palm is down. This can cause an inadvertent disarm by prying the baton from the officers grip on impact. Ensuring proper hand position helps make sure that opposite pressure travelling down the baton and into the hand is absorbed into the strongest part of the grip and palm of the hand.
3. The third most common mistake is for officers to start pulling the baton back to a ready position before all of the force from the strike goes into the target. Help officers to push the tip of the baton into the target to begin the cycle back to a ready position instead of simply pulling their hand back.
4. Watch for use of body mechanics, particularly foot, hip, and shoulder rotation.
5. Help participants aim with the butt of the baton before striking. This helps keep the path the tip of the baton travels along short which makes it harder for subject's to counter.

Technique #4. Forehand and Backhand Blocking Strikes

1. The most common mistake is floating the baton between the officer and subject and using wrist mechanics to strike. Make sure trainees are fully cycling the baton from the Open

to Closed ready positions and back. The helps with retention and generating force into a strike.
2. Watch for use of body mechanics, particularly foot, hip, and shoulder rotation.
3. Help participants aim with the butt of the baton before striking. This helps keep the path the tip of the baton travels along short which makes it harder for subject's to counter.

Technique #5. Closed Mode Butt Strike

1. Make sure participants are covering the tip of the baton with their thumb when delivering the strikes with the butt cap.
2. Watch for use of body mechanics, particularly foot, hip, and shoulder rotation.
3. Make sure trainees are fully cycling the baton from the Open to Closed ready positions and back. The helps with retention and generating force into a strike.

> **Module 10. Takedowns**
>
> In many force altercations an officer's goal is to acquire a dominant position over the subject. The most effective of these positional relationships is with a subject lying on the ground on their front (Prone Position) and an officer standing on their feet.
>
> This for this reason it is critical that officers have an understanding of how to effectively control and disrupt a subject's balance.

Chapter Testing Objectives

1. Demonstrate an understanding of Balance.
2. Demonstrate the different techniques for disrupting a subject's' balance.

Understanding Balance.

Before practicing how to engage a subject with a takedown technique, it's important to have a conceptual understanding of their application, effects, and limitations.

Balance manipulation is a principle that relies on disrupting the natural homeostatic state between the relationship between the head, shoulders, hips, knees, and ankles. This can be accomplished two ways; one use of the limbs as levers, and two disrupting spinal alignment by attacking the core of the subject.

With both methods it is critical to understand the most likely outcome of the technique to predict when and where a subject is going fall. Both methods can be accomplished with striking or pushing energy.

In this chapter only spinal disruption techniques are examined. For examples of leverage techniques see **Module 7 Control Holds**.

Disrupting Balance

Technique #1. Horizontal Rear Jaw Control

- Jaw control is otherwise referred to as Head Manipulation or Jaw Manipulation
- Jaw control can be accomplished in several ways. Imagine that the subject sees the world calculated on two planes, a horizontal and a vertical. By manipulating the mandible (jaw) the officer is able to manipulate where the eyes look in relation to those 2 planes.
- A rear horizontal jaw control is performed from the ambush position with the officer behind the subject. It is often used to overcome handcuff resistance, stop a fleeing subject, or ambush a subject who's engaged with a 3rd party in front of them.

- The technique starts by the officer extending their hands past the subject's head and clasping them together one over the other.
- The officer begins to pull their hands back to them catching the subject across the bridge of the nose and across the eyes.
- The officer then strikes down into the subject's' shoulder blades with their elbows.
- The officer finishes the technique by flaring their elbows up and to the side while pushing down forcing the subject to land on their back. Remember "head to heels" and push straight down not back into you.
- The officer must take into account space requirements and decide whether or not to stay still, step sideways or straight back while the subject is falling.

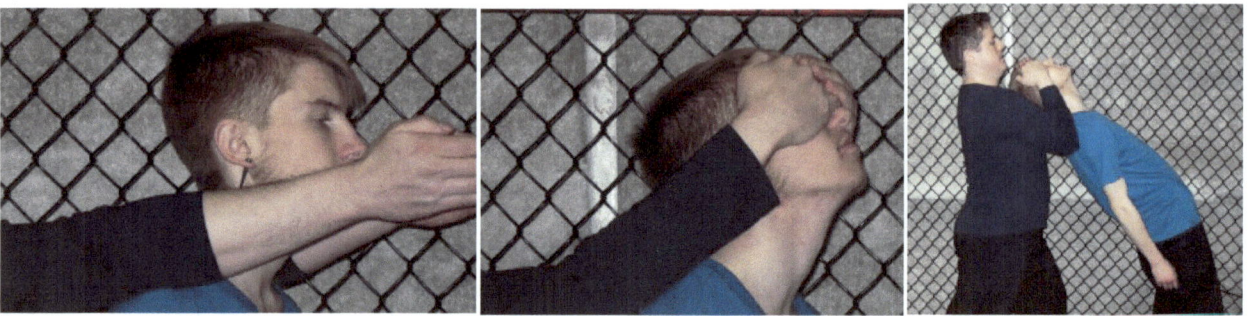

Technique #2. Horizontal Front Jaw Control

- A front horizontal jaw control is performed from the inside position with the officer in front the subject. It is often used to overcome rear jaw control resistance, or when fighting from the inside position.
- The technique starts by the officer clinching their hands behind the subject's head and clasping them together one over the other.
- The officer begins to pull their hands forewords and down to direct the subject's eyes to the ground.
- The officer finishes the technique by flaring their elbows up and to the side while pushing down forcing the subject to land on their stomach. Remember "nose to toes" and push straight down not forewords into you.
- The officer must take into account space requirements and decide whether or not to stay still, step sideways, straight down or straight back while the subject is falling.

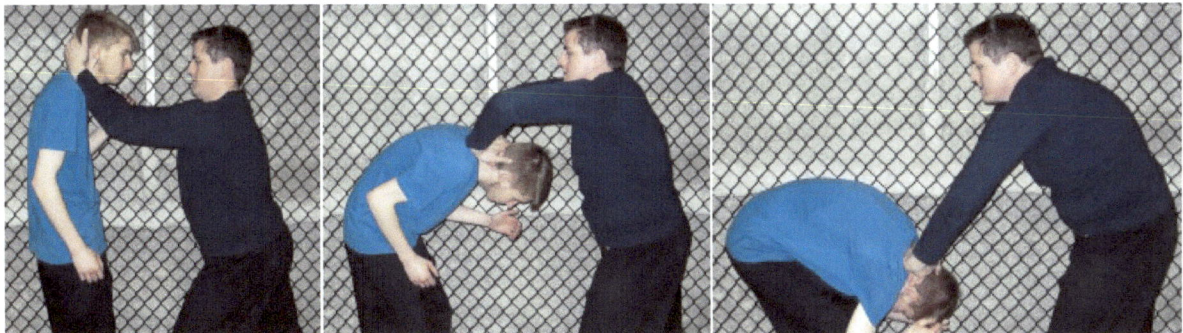

Technique #3. Shoulder and Knee Manipulation

- If the subject is too tall relative to the officer for a Rear Horizontal Jaw Manipulation then the Rear Shoulder Pull with Knee Push technique can be used.
- A Rear Shoulder Pull with Knee Push is performed from the ambush position with the officer behind the subject. It is often used to overcome handcuff resistance, stop a fleeing subject, or ambush a subject who's engaged with a 3rd party in front of them.
- The technique starts by the officer grabbing the subject's' shoulders at the trapezoids while simultaneously placing one foot on the back of the subject's mirror side leg with toes pointing out.

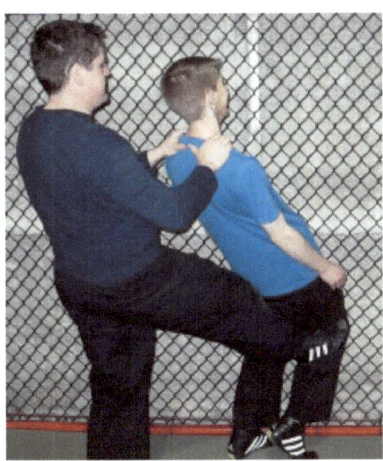

- The officer begins to pull their hands back to them pulling the subject shoulders back while simultaneously pushing out into the subject's' knee. THIS IS NOT A KICK but rather must be a push.
- The officer finishes the technique by flaring their elbows up and to the side while pushing down forcing the subject to land on their back. Remember "head to heels" and push straight down not back into you.
- The officer must take into account space requirements and decide whether or not to stay still, step sideways or straight back while the subject is falling.

Module 10 Conclusion

The effectiveness of attempting to disrupt a subject's balance is never guaranteed. Subject's vary a great deal in terms of how well they maintain or recover balance. Officers should be comfortable flowing from 1 technique to another and executing techniques from a variety of situations and positions.

Balance Disruption techniques are generally completed as Goal #3, Finish the Fight. Officers must also remember there are several things to take into account before attempting to disrupt a subject's balance such as the size and apparent strength of a subject, any observable health risks posed by the subject, and if the officer has the space to move in.

Instructor Notes

Technique #1. Horizontal Rear Jaw Control

1. Watch for attendees interlacing their fingers together. This bad habit can allow subject's to reach up and grab and control both hands.
2. Hands too high or too low over the subject's face will either allow the subject greater resistance by engaging neck muscles OR in the case of too high the officers hands have a greater chance of slipping off the top of the subject's head.
3. Some participants will attempt to pull back on the subject head instead of stabilizing it and moving the subject's' shoulders.
4. Some participants struggle with lateral movement as the subject falls. Be sure to demonstrate tipping points of balance and once the subject is falling let them go and move sideways out of the way.
5. Some people pull their subject straight back against their chest instead of manipulating the jaw.

Technique #2. Horizontal Front Jaw Control

1. Watch for attendees interlacing their fingers together. This bad habit can allow subject's to reach up and grab and control both hands.
2. Some participants will attempt to pull forwards on the subject's head instead of manipulating their head until the eyes are downwards and then pushing down on the back of the head.
3. Some people pull their subject straight forwards into a tackle.

Technique #3. Shoulder and Knee Manipulation

1. The most common mistake is for participants to kick the back of the subject's' knee instead of push into it. A kick will not effectively disrupt balance because the subject's' leg will return to its normal position as soon as the force cycles off the target.
2. The second most common mistake is for people to twist their hips and point the toes inwards or straight up. Be sure to discuss hip alignment and surface area and help participants learn to keep their toes out.

3. Some participants struggle with lateral movement as the subject falls. Be sure to demonstrate tipping points of balance and once the subject is falling let them go and move sideways out of the way.
4. Some people pull their subject straight back against their chest instead of pulling the subject down.
5. Watch for sound body mechanics such as pulling down with the legs not the back and not crossing feet when moving laterally.

> ## Module 11. Inside Position Combatives
>
> In police combatives the Inside Position is often taught as a position to avoid. Instead outside positions, often referred to as level II ½, and sought and taught to be more desirable. While an outside position does have certain tactical advantages it also poses 2 problems. The first is how does an officer get to the outside when an opponent is actively assaulting them? In some instances if the officer is too focused on seeking the outside position they may be prolonging their exposure to the assault instead of fighting back and ending the encounter. The second problem with the outside position during an assault is that it limits the officers' ability to strike targets which may allow more expedient control of the subject and an end to the assault.

Chapter Testing Objectives

1. Demonstrate the Leg Reap Takedown.
2. Demonstrate the Windmill Takedown.

Understanding the Inside Position.

The inside position is defined as, "the position an officer occupies, relative to a subject, that is within a step and arms reach and directly in front of the subject."
This position is often thought to be dangerous because the subject can attack with hands, feet, knees, elbows, spitting, biting, and head butting (highlighted in yellow). What's often forgotten however is that the officer has the same weapon delivery systems available to them (highlighted in white), with the exception of spitting and biting which is only appropriate in very extreme lethal force circumstances.

While an outside position offers protection from an assailant's weapon delivery systems and allows an officer to use theirs it also limits the targets available AND can be almost impossible to get to in a real life altercation. An assailant will naturally attempt to keep their target directly in front of them to attack them with these weapon delivery systems.

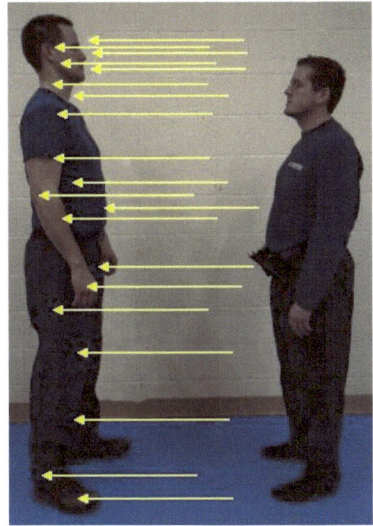

It's important to keep in mind that for an officer the subject's most desirable and incapacitating targets are available from the inside position. Each arrow in figure 2 represents one of the following targets; eyes, nose, ears, mouth, side of the neck, wind pipe/throat, shoulder, bicep, elbow, forearm, wrist/hand/fingers, floating ribs, solar plexus, groin, thigh (inside & outside), knee, shin, ankle, and foot. As you can see with training and practice an officer who can control this position can develop the skill to be quite effective at controlling an assaultive subject in varying degrees of violence and danger.

Inside Position Combatives

Technique 1. Stopping the Initial Strike

- As the subject attacks with a hook punch step into the attack and raise both arms.

 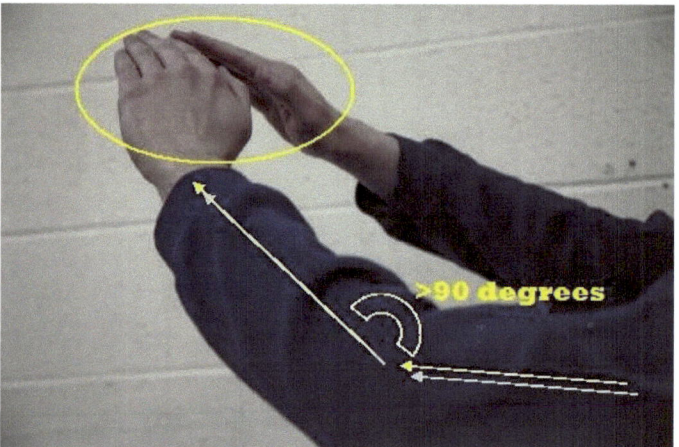

- Contact is made with the bony ridge of the hand or forearm. Fingers are cupped together for protection and contact is made on the forearm with one hand to stop the weapon from contacting the target and high into the bicep, shoulder, or chest to stop the forward momentum of the assailant.

- Once the officer has effectively stopped the initial impact of the weapon the second step is to stop that weapon from being able to cycle and attack again. To do this the officer wraps their far arm over the attacking arm, pins the attackers hand into their armpit, and wraps their fingers around the base of the triceps digging into the bony protrusions where the radius and ulna connect to the humorous.

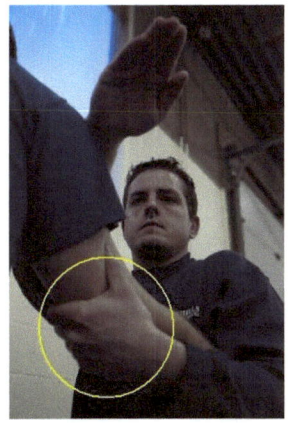
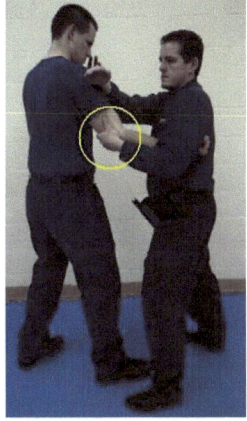

- Once the subject's arm is effectively wrapped and controlled facilitation and thought interruption strikes are encouraged. The best options are either a forearm strike to the side of the neck or a hammer fist strike to the side of the jaw. In a lethal force situation eye rakes, throat strikes or grabs, and knee strikes to the groin are all effective options.

- Once control is established on the arm that attacked, the officers' free arm applies upwards pressure into the jaw of the subject. Simultaneously the officer draws down on the elbow with the grabbing hand and arm. This will force the subject's' eyes up and thereby break their balance to the rear. This position stops the subject from being able to effectively attack and allows the officer to drive in closer to the subject for the Leg Reap Takedown.

Technique #2. Leg Reap Takedown

- Once control is established and an opportunity presents itself the officer then brings their inside leg forward and behind the subject to swing it back and between the subject's legs. The term "Leg Reap" is used to illustrate to officers that this is a violent action.
- The Reap from the leg is from the hip and takes the foot in a **straight line** through the subject's' center effectively kicking out one leg.

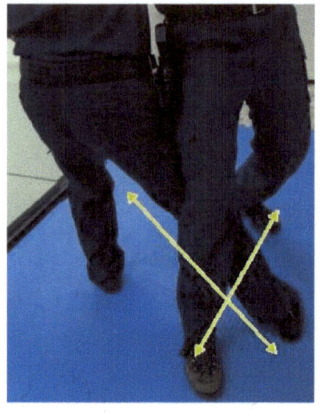 

- This motion combined with the force being applied to the subject's' jaw tilting their head back takes their balance and forces them to fall to the ground.

Technique #3. Windmill Takedown

- In the case where the opponent attacks "Boxer Style" the leg corresponding with their attacking arm may be rearwards. In this case reaching for the leg reap will likely put the officer off balance and prolong the encounter. As with the leg reap steps 1-3 are the same. For the rearwards position however officers change techniques and utilize the Windmill Takedown.
- To initiate the Windmill takedown the officer takes control of the back of the subject's head and pulls down instead of pushing up as in the Leg Reap. The best place to grip is at the base of the skull/top of the neck. The natural bony protrusions allow for a good grip at this location.

- The next step is to compromise the subject's' base by kicking the inside of their far knee with the flat of the foot. By pointing the toes out the officer is able to maximize surface area and increase their chances of affecting the target in a dynamic confrontation.
- Once the subject's balance has been compromised the officer completes the Windmill takedown by pulling up and pushing the subject's head under on the control arm. Officers must make sure they move out of the way or else the subject will run into their legs perhaps initiating a new attack.

Module 11 Conclusion

In a violent altercation officers are usually responding to a sudden attack and often don't even know the nature of the attack. While getting to an outside position offers more safety from incoming strikes it can be very difficult to acquire. People who are attacking will keep trying to align themselves to a target. In a violent assault it takes great skill and technical ability to maintain an outside position relative to an attacker.

It is therefore necessary for officers to become comfortable fighting from the position they're most likely to find themselves in. Developing a key set of strategies and techniques can keep an officer safe and allow them to control the situation accordingly.

Instructor Notes

1. In step 1 of the training progression the trainee role playing the assaultive subject will only attack with wide angle hook punches. This is to allow their training partner an opportunity to learn and become comfortable with the material. It's important to note that if the officer doesn't move or block the attack the subject's hand MUST touch the side of their jaw.
2. As participants advance in skill change the hook punch to a straight punch to make the drills more challenging.

Technique #1. Stopping the Initial Strike

1. Remember to illustrate to trainees the importance of extending arms past 90 degrees to create structural integrity. It may be necessary to introduce a drill where they stand in front of their training partner with their forearms less than 90 degrees to their upper arm and their partner collapses the arm. Then repeat the drill with their arms extended past 90 degrees and let them experience how much stronger that position is.
2. Watch to make sure participants fingers are cupped together for protection.
3. It is a common mistake either grab the assailant's forearm OR for the officer to use their forearm to attempt to hook the subject. Either one of these errors will allow for the subject to pull their arm free and continue attacking with that arm.

Technique #2. Leg Reap Takedown

1. The most common mistake is that officers will plant their leg and try to push subject's over it.
2. The second most common mistake is twisting or turning during this process
3. The third problem trainee's encounter is moving their feet to keep up with the subject as they fall and adopting the power squat position. Some participants will be tempted to let go of the arm and allow the subject to fall away from them. Illustrate the takedown with edged weapons and firearms to illustrate the importance of maintaining control of the weapon arm.

Technique #3. Windmill Takedown

1. The most common mistake is for participants to attempt to twist their hips and side kicks the subject's' leg to affect their base. Be sure to demonstrate and watch for the toes out principle.
2. The second most common mistake is for people to not move their feet during the takedown and pull the subject into a tackle at their legs.
3. The third problem trainee's encounter is moving their feet to keep up with the subject as they fall and adopting the power squat position. Some participants will be tempted to let go of the arm and allow the subject to fall away from them. Illustrate the takedown with edged weapons and firearms to illustrate the importance of maintaining control of the weapon arm.

> **Module 12. Ground Fighting**
>
> In an encounter a Ground Fight can be a extremely dangerous thing. Officers must understand the importance of understanding how to defend against a takedown attempt and, if the confrontation goes to the ground, understand the positions and corresponding transitions that will allow them mobility and an opportunity to fight back and protect themselves.

Chapter Testing Objectives

1. Explain the unique factors that make ground fights so dangerous
2. Demonstrate the Sprawl and Jaw manipulation takedown defenses
3. Demonstrate the Bridge when a subject is on mount
4. Demonstrate a scissor sweep when a subject is in guard
5. Demonstrate a scissor kick reversal when a subject is on rear mount
6. Demonstrate a back door escape when a subject is on side control
7. Demonstrate shrimping and standing sweeps
8. Demonstrate breakdancer escape when a subject has north-south position

Understanding the Ground Fight Scenario

A ground fight is seen first and foremost as a violent dangerous assault against an officer. The reasons are listed below;

1. In a ground fight situation more kinetic energy is delivered from strikes due to the nature of stomping and kicking and the fact that counter pressure increases the transfer of kinetic energy into the officers' body through movement.
2. In a ground fight situation whoever maintains the top position can generate more power and use less energy by striking with gravity and body mechanics.
3. The person on the bottom position quiet often can't reach the person with the top position with strikes due to body mechanics
4. In a ground fight situation an officer will likely be limited as to what weapons they can access to control the subject.
5. Subject's generally become more violent once a fight hits the ground.
6. If an officer is on the bottom position they don't have the option of disengagement.
7. Moving on the ground requires more energy to overcome friction.
8. Moving on the ground may cause dirt and debris to become lodged in an officers equipment thereby causing malfunctions or it may tear and rip equipment and remove it from the officers belt.
9. An officer's ability to deal with multiple opponent's is drastically limited while on the ground.

For the reasons listed above officers must train mentally and physically to treat a ground fight assault as a dangerous situation that requires immediate action. The program is broken into 3 categories; preventing the take down, defending against a standing opponent, grappling with a grounded opponent.

Technique 1. Sprawl and Matador

- As opponent attempts a tackle shoot hips back
- Forearms simultaneously strike the opponent's shoulders and press into the opponent's jaw
- Push off opponent to stay standing and adjust angle to opponent
- Remember to illustrate that the primary control is from **JAW CONTROL**, not the actual sprawl of the hips.

Technique #2. Sprawl to Back Control

- As opponent attempts a tackle shoot hips back
- Forearms simultaneously strike the opponent's shoulders and press into the opponent's jaw
- Shoot hips back
- Forearms simultaneously strike the supra scapular nerve motor point
- "Ride" opponent to the ground and move to back mount position

Technique #3. 1 leg trap release

- From a failed sprawl the opponent manages to wrap up 1 leg
- Officer strikes down on back of the head with hammer fist or elbow strikes and pushes down on the back of the head while dropping body weight.
- Officer shoots hand down along body between their body and opponent's head

- Officer curls arm up over opponent's face (be sure to discuss why not the neck) to begin jaw manipulation
- Officer clasps hands together and utilizes a step and body twist to complete jaw manipulation takedown

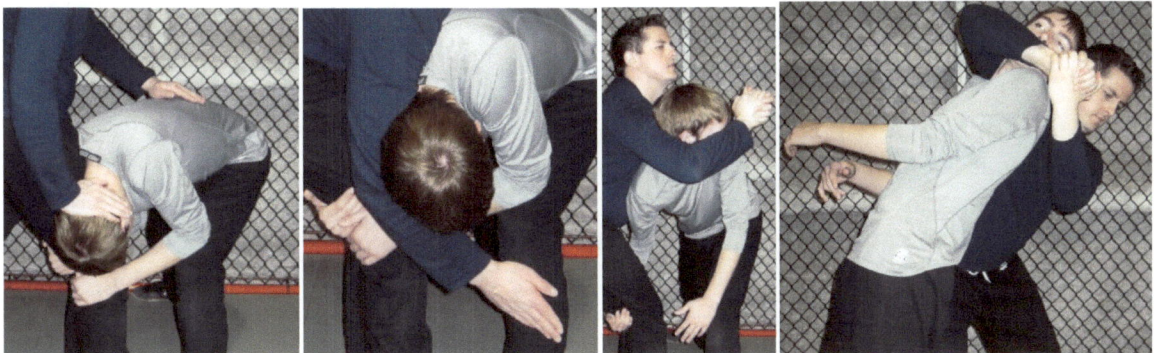

Technique #4. Back ground fight position

- The Rear Ground Fight Position is when an officer is lying flat on their back with their head up off the ground and hands in front of them protecting their head and face. One foot is on the ground and the other is in the air but tucked in close to the body.
- It is important to keep both feet tucked close to the body to prevent an assailant from grabbing the feet/ankles and pulling the legs out of the way to get on top of the officer.
- The officer uses the foot on the ground to turn and keep their feet pointed at their opponent in the case where the opponent is trying to get around the officer and get on top of them.

- From this position the officer can use Thrust Kicks to the opponent's shins and lower legs to keep them away.
- Often times when kicked hard below the knee people will bend forwards at the waist. In circumstances where lethal force is reasonable and necessary an officer may kick upwards at the opponent's face and head.

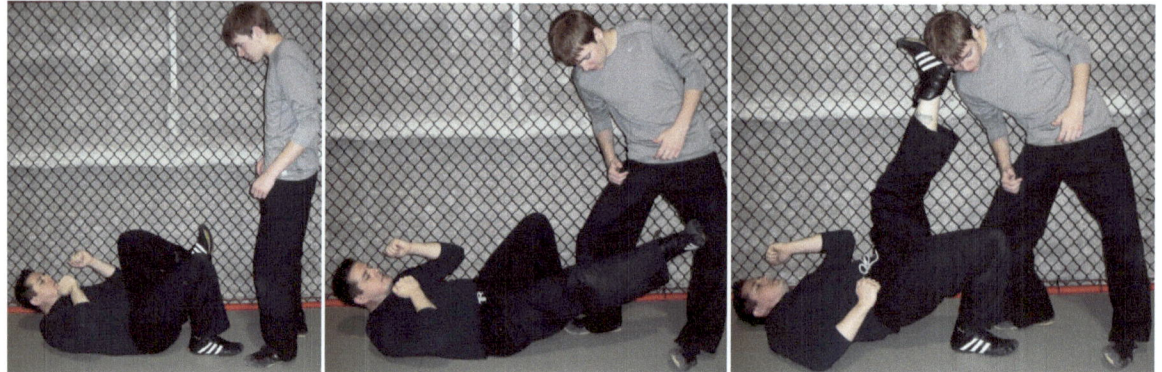

- If the opportunity presents itself the officer may use the Knee Bar to knock the opponent backwards to the ground. The knee bar is performed by first rolling onto 1 side and then using that foot to trap behind the opponent's ankle with the top of the foot. Next the free (elevated) leg pushes up and into the knee thereby locking it extended. Continue to apply force and the leg will become a long lever to the hips knocking the opponent down.

Technique #5. Shrimping

- Shrimping is used to create space and angular movement while lying on the ground.

- To complete a shrimp the officer digs the balls of their feet into the ground and lifts their hips up. Next they swing their pelvis to one side as they turn onto their other side and looks towards their own feet.

- From an opponent in their guard the officer can shrimp to bring 1 shin across the subject's body. From here they can push off the subject to create space, return to the rear ground fight position, and apply kicks to keep the assailant off of them.

Technique #6. Getting back to standing from the ground

- From the rear ground fight position the officer can sit up and use 1 hand to assist them to get to a 3-point posture. From the 3 point posture both hands are used to protect their head and face as they finish standing up.

Technique #7. Bridging when subject on full mount

- The full mount is when the officer is lying on their back and an opponent is straddled on their chest with their knees on the ground. It is considered the second most dangerous position in ground fighting.
- To begin the officer must make sure the assailant can't strike down with their hands. While it may be possible to grab their wrists this likely won't work because the assailant has such a positional advantage they can free their wrists. Therefore the better option is to strike up into the opponent's tail bone with a knee while simultaneously bridging the hips up and forwards. This will cause the opponent to lean and fall forwards making them put their hands out to catch their fall.
- Next the officer grabs a hold of an elbow much like when performing a standing trap and traps the ankle of the same side with the back of their leg or foot. This prevents the

opponent on top from posting their limbs out or posturing up back to the straddle position.
- Next the officer bridges their hips up and rolls to the same side that they have trapped. When performed correctly the officer will finish on their knees in the opponent's guard.

Technique #8. Scissor sweep when subject in guard

- There are several benefits to holding the guard in a ground altercation. Primarily it uses the legs and strong arm position to hold the subject tight so that they can't create the space necessary to accelerate a strike. An officer can't hold a subject indefinitely in guard however. Particularly in the case of multiple opponent's.

- To pull guard an officer must be sure to wrap the legs around the subject just above their hips and sit up to grab them. The best way to grab with the hands is on the back of the subject's head and their right elbow. Pull them into the core and hold them there to prevent being struck.

- When an officer detects an opening they can reverse the position using the Scissor Sweep. While maintaining an elbow trap the officer opens the guard and shrimping to get one leg flat to the ground. This leg is used to disrupt the subject's posting leg from the knee (using back of the leg and foot methods) and then scissor sweeping to the mount by pushing into the subject's ribs and core with their other knee.

 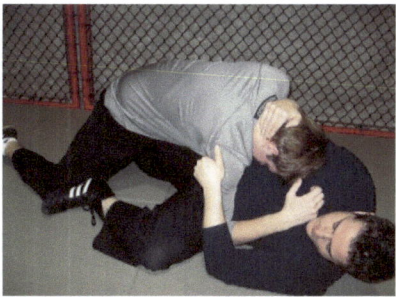 

Technique #9. Scissor Kick Reversal when subject on rear mount

- The first priority when an opponent is on the Rear Mount is to protect the back of the head from strikes and the neck from a choke. This is done by shrugging the shoulders and clasping the back of the head with both hands.

- Immediately after protecting the back of the head and neck officers should use the scissor kick escape and scramble with jaw pressure to side control. This is done by digging the hips into the ground so that the subject can't wrap their legs around and hold on and violently scissor kicking the legs, one over and one under the other, to rotate the hips. If the subject falls onto their side then the officer reaches up and uses jaw control to push their head away as they scramble to the side. Once side control is established the officer can continue to engage by using the knee on belly transition to mount.
- If there is space between the officer and subject during the Scissor Kick then they might roll under the subject and finish with the subject on their front mount. From here the officer uses the bridge.

Technique #10. Scrambling when Officer in Guard

- In the case of an officer in the subject's the guard a guard break can be used. First however base and control must be established. This is accomplished by the officer using jaw control to sit back seat to heels, posture high with knees wide to control base and hands to subject's stomach
- Next the officer walks their knee over to line up with subject's tail bone and re establish base with other knee under subject's leg. This in combination with elbow pressure into the inner thigh and strikes is necessary will eventually open the subject's guard.
- Once the guard is open bring the far knee over the subject's leg to pin it to the ground and prevent them from wrapping a leg with theirs.

- From this position the other leg can be brought out and side control can be established. If the officer decides to continue to engage then the knee on belly method of getting on the mount can be used.

Technique #11. Breakdancer Reversal when Officer in North-South

- North-South occurs when the officer and subject are facing each other on the ground. This position can refer to many different methods in which this can happen. In a law enforcement situation however this is most likely to occur when both parties are on their knees and the subject either wraps the officers neck for a headlock or wraps around their body.

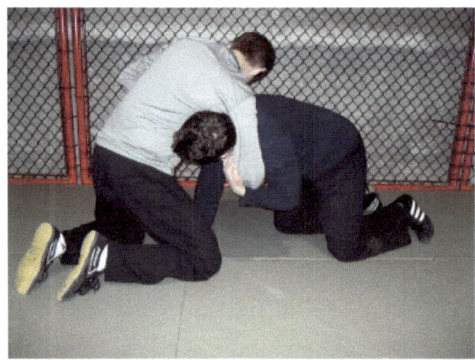

- From this position the officer must utilize angles. To do this first the officer decides which side they're going to attempt to escape on. This is generally decided by which side of the subject's body the head side of the officers head is pressed against.
- Once this is decided the officer uses an arm to control the subject's hands and, in the case of a headlock, looks into the subject's ribs. Next the officer postures up on the far knee and arm and begins establishing their escape angle by opening their leg on the side they're going to escape to.

- Next the officer brings their far leg through the opening they created and pressures back into the subject's' ribs with the back of their head while simultaneously sitting onto their buttock.

- From this position the officer can continue to engage by scissoring their legs and maintaining back pressure into the subject. They will either end on side control (if the subject landed supine) or on back mount (if the subject landed prone).

Technique #12. Back Door Escapes

- In certain situations an officer can't move a subject. In these situations a transition method known as "Back Door Escape" is utilized. The concept of the back door escape can be utilized from any position where the subject is on top and the officer is supine.
- To utilize the Back Door Escape from a failed bridge maintain hip elevation and inserting one arm below the subject's' inner thigh.
- Use the inserted arm to create pressure over the head as hips fall back into the space and legs pull the officer from under the subject behind them. Turn to face the subject.

Technique #13. Twisting arm control when Officer on Mount

- Once full mount is established Twisting Arm control is the preferred method to establish a handcuffing position. First use strikes for encourage the subject to cover their head and face.
- Next use the two-on-one arm control to angle subject's arm across their own jaw

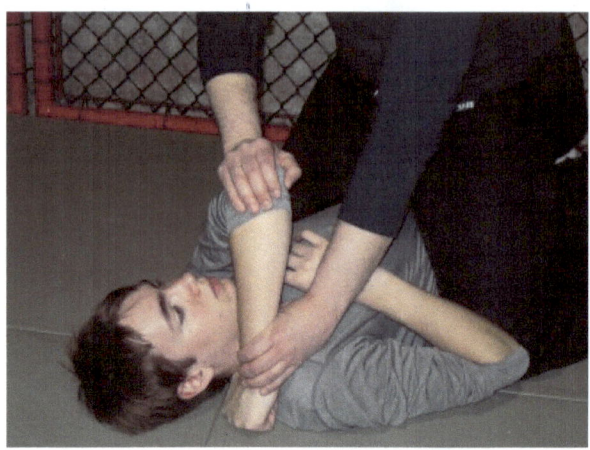 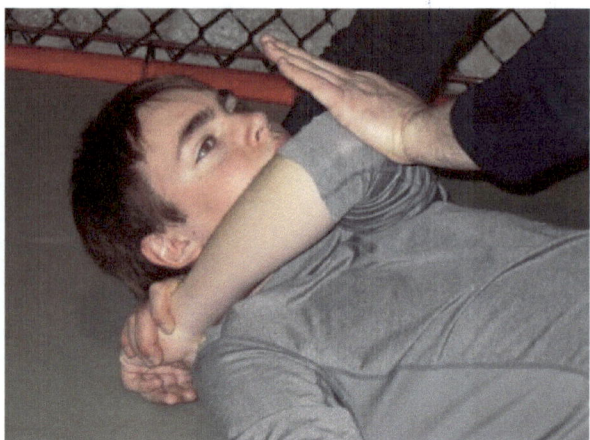

- Use body control to keep it there while establishing behind the head control
- Posture to a 3 point posture while pulling up on the subject's wrist with arm behind their head and down on their elbow. Remember that power comes from the use hips

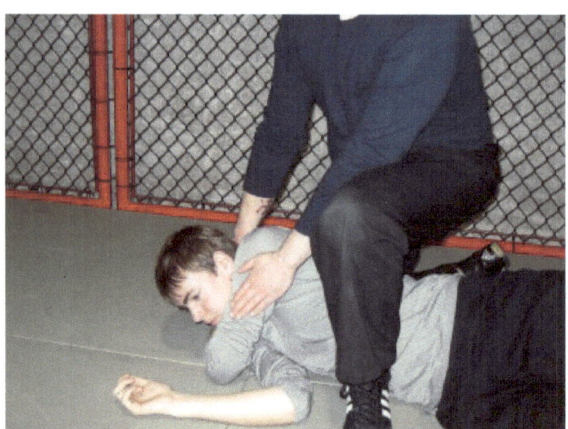

- Establish rear mount.

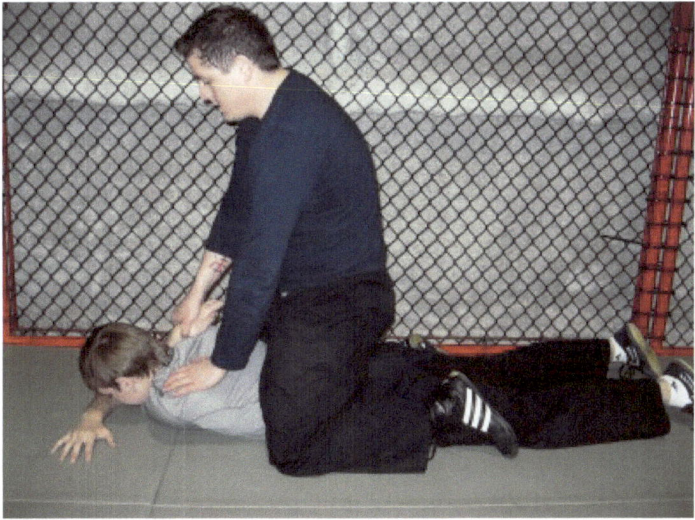

- From rear mount 2-on-1 arm control and hammer lock can be used to establish the handcuffing position. Agencies trained in the use of neck restraints can also apply one here.

Technique #14. Incorporating body weapons and duty weapons

- There are various ways to officers to incorporate their technological weapons into ground fighting. Some general examples are included below.
- OC Spray deployed into palm of the hand from in belt and jaw control becomes an OC Face Wash
- Deployed baton used for body control on lower ribs or elbow control
- Keeping firearm tucked to chest while using legs to move and maintain corner
- Side shrimp shooting platform
- Supine shooting platform
- Shooting subject while they're in officers guard
- Shooting subject while they're on another person's mount or rear mount
- Incorporating jaw control into all transitions
- Incorporating eye gauges and trachea control into all transitions
- Incorporate elbow lockdown when subject is on officers mount trying to access weapons on duty belt before making transitions
- From officer on mount using the ground as an environmental weapon to strike subject's head against

Module 12 Conclusion

In a violent altercation officers are usually responding to a sudden attack and often don't even know the nature of the attack. Ground fights are very violent and dangerous confrontations. Officers therefore must be comfortable responding, moving, and transitioning on the ground.
Instructor Notes

1. In ground fight training quit often new students will waste energy by being frantic and panicked. One of the goals to help them understand the realities of these confrontations and be confident enough to relax, think about what's happening, and execute their techniques with smooth body movement.
2. Start each technique with no resistance from the training partner and gradually increase the resistance and partners responses as their skill increases.
3. Show students how to drill each movement without a partner and if time permits warm up with the solo drills after every break.

Technique #1. Sprawl and Matador

1. Make sure to emphasize the importance of jaw control and have the students practice with their backs against a wall or other obstruction to illustrate the importance or jaw control and forwards angular movement.

Technique #2. Sprawl to Back Control

1. Watch to make sure students are effectively securing the back of the subject's head and driving down with their hips by arching their back. One thing that can help beginners it to look up with the eyes.

Technique #3. 1 leg trap release

1. The most common mistake is to interlace the fingers instead of using a snowball or Gable grip.
2. Watch to make sure students are using their legs and core to effect the release and maintaining balance throughout.

Technique #4. Back ground fight position

1. The back ground fight position can be difficult with duty equipment. Make sure to have students wear their equipment after they become comfortable with the basics.
2. Some new students will have a tendency to leave 1 foot floating away from their core. When this happens have the subject role-player grab and pull on it. Also watch to make sure that officer students are holding their head up off the ground.
3. Watch students and ensure that when they're kicking the strikes follow a straight line and not a bicycle kick.

Technique #5. Shrimping

1. Make sure to have students practice shrimping in a variety of situations including against walls, when subject's are standing over them striking, and when subject's are in their guard.
2. Have the students practice shrimping in their full equipment so that they learn to lift their hips before attempting the shrimp.

Technique #6. Getting back to standing from the ground

1. Officers should be able to maintain their balance while getting up off the ground and use their legs to lift themselves up while continuing to circumnavigate. If their posture is crossed or their eyes aren't up correct the technique.

Technique #7. Bridging when subject on full mount

1. The number one error when bridging happens when students lift their hips at the beginning of the movement but then allow them to fall when executing the roll. Watch students and be sure to correct this error as soon as it happens. IF students are still struggling have their subject role-player allow them to roll underneath them between their legs and take rear mount to illustrate why the hips must remain elevated throughout the movement.

Technique #8. Scissor sweep when subject in guard

1. A lot of students struggle getting their kicking leg low to the ground and end up striking or pushing into the subject thigh or hips. This can render the technique ineffective because this is where the subject's strong. To make sure their getting their leg to drive on the subject's knee emphasize the importance of the shrimp and build in the tactile reference of their leg scraping the ground as they drive on the subject's posting leg.

Technique #9. Scissor Kick Reversal when subject on rear mount

1. If officers lift their hips when the subject is on their back it wastes energy and allows subject's the ability to wrap their legs around the midsection or inside the thighs. If this happens it can be nearly impossible to escape. For this reason ensure that officers drill the scissor kick reversal before attempting with a partner. If they lift their hips once their practicing the drill have their training partner wrap the legs around them.
2. As soon as the officers hips and shoulders rotate and they're free of the subject have them immediately scramble to a dominant position OR their feet.
3. As students skill and confidence increases have the subject role-player posture up for strikes and allow the officer to roll under them. Once they finish rolling their partner will be on their mount. Have them immediately execute the bridge.

Technique #10. Scrambling when Officer in Guard

1. The most common mistake is for students to try to rely on pain control or strength to open the subject's guard.
2. Make sure they are using their posture and kneeling base to manipulate their opponent's' legs and open the guard.
3. Also ensure that officers are bringing their far leg across the subject guard to prevent the trapping of their legs. As their skill and confidence increases instruct training partners to

wrap both legs around one of the officers legs if the officer doesn't execute the escape properly.

Technique #11. Breakdancer Reversal when Officer in North-South

1. Make sure students understand how to bury their face into the subject's ribs to protect against a choking headlock.
2. If officers are struggling maintaining back pressure teach them how to use their eyes to look up behind them to maintain the head-pressure into the subject.
3. As soon as the subject loses balance make sure the officers are scrambling to a dominant position or standing position.

Technique #13. Twisting arm control when Officer on Mount

1. Sometimes officers will have a tendency to over rotate the subject thereby giving them enough energy to continue moving and possibly escaping the control hold. One of the solutions to this problem are to keep their legs tight to the subject when they posture up.
2. When transitioning to the handcuffing position demonstrate how to use the arm counter pressure method to force the subject's hand to the rear hammer lock.
3. From the hammer lock demonstrate how to create pressure in the subject shoulder to encourage them to pass their free hand back to the small of their back.
4. If incorporating neck restraints ensure to cover the risk of subject fatality due to cross arm pressure from the nature of the position. Demonstrate how to fix this with the support hand.

> **Module 13. Strikes**
>
> There has been, and continues to be much controversy surrounding the idea of striking a subject. It is thought that public perception looks unfavorably upon strikes because it appears like they're delivered out of anger, frustration, and panic.
>
> This is not the intended motivation behind striking a subject. Rather strikes are used for two primary reasons. First they distract the subject from staying strong in their structure and joints opening a window for follow up skeletal control, and second they give the officer an entry into establishing position and posture from which they can deploy follow up control methods.

Chapter Testing Objectives

1. Explain the motivation behind striking a subject.
2. Demonstrate the Straight Punch.
3. Demonstrate the Palm Heel Strike.
4. Demonstrate the 3 Elbow Strikes.
5. Demonstrate the Knee Strike.

Understanding Strikes.

Contrary to popular belief, strikes are an unreliable method of controlling a subject. This is for a variety of reasons. First strikes to control someone primarily rely on a pain response. Because people have a wide spectrum of responses to pain it's unknown how a subject will respond. Secondly striking applies kinetic energy and then cycles off the target thereby not actually controlling anything or limiting a subject's ability to continue to move.

In use of force cases from around the world subject's continue to assault their victims even after receiving multiple strikes. A goal orientated attacker can ignore the pain caused by being struck and continue their violent and illegal action.

For these reasons Blue Guardian does not agree that strikes will cause any type of impairment in a subject's ability to move their body or use their skeletal muscle. The majority of subject's who cease their illegal action due to striking do it because they either choose to because of the pain of the strikes or because they're rendered unconscious.

Understanding how to strike is beneficial for two reasons however.

First it can provide an officer the opportunity to regain their structure and position in a fight. Most attacks against officers are a surprise attack. This often puts the officer behind in terms of reaction time and most often results in them moving rewards. A strike by its very nature moves forwards. For this reason strikes are an effective means of moving forwards again and reestablishing skeletal posture and maintaining balance as well as possibly offsetting the physical and mental balance of the attacker. Secondly striking can create entry points for the officer to make the necessary attachments for follow up methods of skeletal control.

Striking often allows a window of opportunity for follow up control methods because the subject, at least for a brief time, is distracted by the strike.

In a best case scenario after receiving a strike a subject will decide to cease their violent illegal action and stop resisting and fighting.

Technique 1. Straight Punch

- The straight punch is the primary strike in the Blue Guardian Control Tactics System. It is applied with the striking foot forwards (regardless of where weapons are worn) and with a vertical fist. The primary target is a subject's face.
- To begin step forwards and raise the hands to the chest.
- Once the feet have stopped moving thrust the hand forwards maintaining a vertical fist while simultaneously dropping the center of gravity and slightly rotating the upper body from hips to shoulders and keeping the other hand elevated to protect the upper body and face.
- Make contact with a straight wrist and the flat of the fingers and knuckles.
- Push through the target and once the end of the strike is reached cycle the hand back in a straight line to the body.

Technique #2. Palm Heel Strike

- The primary targets for the Palm Heel Strike are the subject's upper chest or face. It is an excellent tool for knocking people back and gaining space. It is applied with the striking foot forwards (regardless of where weapons are worn).
- The delivery of the strike starts the same as the Straight Punch. To begin step forwards and raise the hands to the chest.
- Once the feet have stopped moving thrust the hand forwards. Open the fingers and pull them up and back so that they're pointing at the ceiling. Simultaneously drop the center of gravity and slightly rotating the upper body from hips to shoulders and keeping the other hand elevated to protect the upper body and face. Make contact with the base of the hand (the heel of the palm).

- Push through the target and once the end of the strike is reached cycle the hand back in a straight line to the body.

Technique #3. Hammer Fist

- The primary targets for the Hammer Fist are the subject's face or side of their head. It is primarily a close quarters strike and is primarily used when manipulating a subject's skeleton with the other hand.
- To begin the strike step forwards and raise the arms to the chest in a crossed fashion with the forward arm matching the forward leg and elbows bent.
- To deliver the strike rotate into the target and extend the elbow while dropping the center of gravity and closing the fist tightly while turning it so it's horizontal to the ground.
- Contact is made with the meaty portion of the hand under the pinky finger.

Technique #4. Elbow Strikes

- There are many different ways to utilize elbow Strikes. There are 4 different Elbow Strikes all delivered at close quarters. They are the Outside Horizontal Elbow, the Inside Horizontal Elbow, the Uppercut Vertical Elbow, and the Rear Horizontal Elbow. Targeting is to the subject's head.
- All 4 delivery methods utilize some common concepts. They are body rotation, dropping center of gravity at time of impact, forward foot – forward weapon, and impact with the tip of the elbow.
- To deliver an Outside Horizontal Elbow step forwards and raise the corresponding arm, bent in at the elbow so the hand is touching the chest. Rotate the upper body from the hips through the shoulders while simultaneously dropping the center of gravity. Impact is made with the tip of the elbow and a follow through while balance is maintained.

- To deliver an Inside Horizontal Elbow, begin where the Outside Horizontal Elbow finished. Lean forwards into the target while thrusting the elbow forwards into the target.

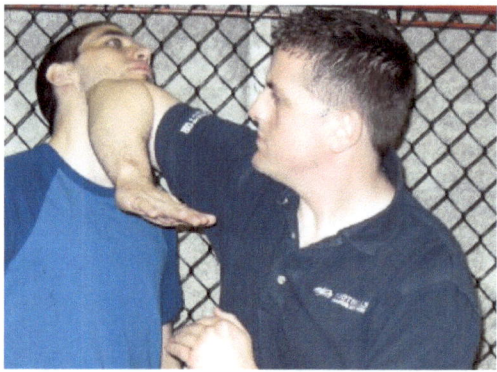

- To deliver a Uppercut Vertical Elbow begin once again by stepping forwards but this time tuck a vertical arm against the rib cage with a bend at the elbow so that the hand is touching the chest. Begin to lift the elbow through the shoulder while simultaneously lifting up onto the ball of the foot and rotating the hips. The primary target is under the subject's chin. Follow through by pointing the elbow straight to the sky.

- To deliver a Rear Horizontal Elbow start by lifting the hands to the chest with elbows bent. Step rearwards with the foot that corresponds with the elbow you wish to strike with. Lift the elbow so that it's horizontal and rotate through the hips and shoulders while dropping the center of gravity. Impact is made with the tip of the elbow.

Technique #5. Knee Strikes

- Knee strikes are primarily used to strike a subject's legs to temporarily alter their base and structure. After a knee strike immediate skeletal manipulation and follow up control should be used.
- To deploy a Knee Strike first ensure a grip with the hands somewhere on the subject's arms or bodies.
- Next chamber the leg intended to apply the strike by stretching it rearwards.
- Deliver the strike by pulling the subject into it using the hands and thrust the tip of the knee through the intended target.
- The most effective target zones are the upper legs.
- Immediately after delivering the strike follow up with a control technique or takedown.

Module 13 Conclusion

While applying strikes to a subject can be beneficial to alter a subject's mental or physical balance, strikes shouldn't be replied on to end a confrontation due to the spectrum of pain tolerance and the unreliability and unpredictability of the effectiveness of the strike.

Strikes should never be delivered out of frustration or retribution but rather should only be applied as part of an overall strategy to manipulate the subject's skeleton and open a window of opportunity for follow up control.

Instructor Notes

Technique #1, 2, and 3.

- There are many common mistakes in the Straight Punch, Palm Heel and Hammer Fist to watch for. They are listed below;
- Rotating the hand to deliver a horizontal fist (Straight Punch) or in the case of the Palm Heel not pulling the fingers up and back to expose the heel of the palm.
- Elbows flared away from body.
- Elbows locking out at the end of the strike.
- Lifting the center of gravity.
- Throwing the body forwards with so much intensity that posture and balance are compromised.
- Not closing the fist tightly (Straight Punch).
- After contact is made failing to follow through OR following through on a new vector.
- Making contact with a limp wrist or a bend in the wrist.
- After contact is made dropping the hand for the return cycle leaving it hang. Remember the thrusting analogy. Straight line in and back (Straight Punch and Palm Heel).

Technique #4.

1. The most common mistakes with elbow strikes are impacting with the forearm, not utilizing body mechanics by rotating hip and either sinking into the strike (with horizontal techniques) or lifting up into the technique (Upper Cut Elbow).

2. Also in the case of the Rear Horizontal Elbow ensure students are looking behind them before striking.

Technique #5. Knee Strikes

1. There three things to watch for when students are learning to apply a knee strike. The first thing is the target zones. Some students will be overly enthusiastic to deliver the strike and won't watch their target. This can result in strikes landing in the groin or stomach which can be inappropriate unless there are particular circumstances.

2. The second most common mistake is not bending the knee enough to expose the tip of the knee and striking with the flat of the thigh.

3. Lastly watch students to ensure they're pulling the subject into the strike to create counter pressure and deliver more force.

> **Module 14. Weapon Retention and Disarming**
>
> It is paramount that officers can not only use their intermediate and lethal weapons effectively BUT be able to retain these weapons as well. If an officer were to lose their weapon not only can it be used against them but members of the public as well.
>
> Remember that armed officers bring weapons into every confrontation, thereby creating the possibility that EVERY encounter is an armed encounter.
>
> Officers must also understand disarming techniques AND the dangers around attempting to disarm a subject. If a disarm is failed or attempted at the wrong time or in inappropriate circumstances the risk of danger to the officer and the public can be drastically increased.

Chapter Testing Objectives

1. Demonstrate retention strategies when a subject is grabbing holstered weapons.
2. Demonstrate retention strategies when a subject is grabbing drawn weapons.
3. Demonstrate disarming techniques.

Understanding Weapon Retention.

Although modern holsters with advanced built in weapon retention devices keep officers safer from having their sidearm taken from them and possibly used against them, weapon retention doesn't just apply to sidearm's, particularly when it comes to equipment on the duty belt.

If a subject is attempting to grab and officers belt OR a lethal or intermediate weapon held in the hand the officer must treat the situation as serious and dangerous and understand how to respond appropriately.

Some control tactics systems advocate responding with strikes and violence Blue Guardian advocates responding with skeletal manipulation methods. A focused attacker can remain goal orientated through the pain that striking causes. Skeletal manipulation however allows officers a greater degree of control and a higher chance of success.

These techniques must applied with speed, commitment, and violence.

Technique #1. Subject Grabs Holstered Firearm Mirror Side

- Lock the subject's elbow it prevents them from deploying the weapon from the holster. To do this the officer wraps their arm over the attacking arm, pins the attackers hand into their armpit, and wraps their fingers around the base of the triceps digging into the bony protrusions where the radius and ulna connect to the humorous.

- Once the subject's arm is effectively wrapped and controlled facilitation and thought interruption strikes are encouraged. The best options are either a forearm strike to the side of the neck or a hammer fist strike to the side of the jaw. Because of the lethality of the situation eye rakes, throat strikes or grabs, and knee strikes to the groin are all effective options.

- Once control is established on the arm that attacked, the officers' free arm applies upwards pressure into the jaw of the subject. Simultaneously the officer draws down on the elbow with the grabbing hand and arm. This will force the subject's' eyes up and thereby break their balance to the rear. This position stops the subject from being able to effectively attack and allows the officer to drive in closer to the subject for the Leg Reap Takedown.

- In the case of a double hand grab follow the same sequence.

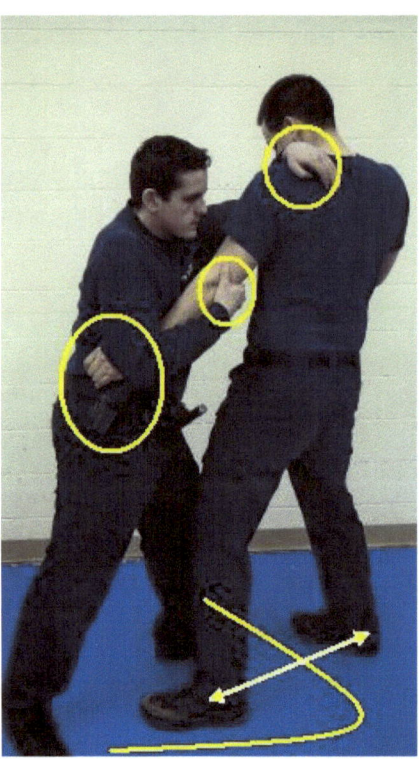

Technique #2. Subject Grabs Holstered Firearm Cross Side

- In the case of a cross body gun grab the sequence starts out the same as illustrated above. However as the officer moves into the subject to take their space and center line they will actually end up on the outside of the subject.
- The officer wraps their dominant arm over the attacking arm, pins the attackers hand into their armpit, and wraps their fingers around the base of the triceps digging into the bony protrusions where the radius and ulna connect to the humorous.

- Once the subject's arm is effectively wrapped and controlled facilitation and thought interruption strikes are encouraged. The best options are either a forearm strike to the side of the neck or a hammer fist strike to the side of the jaw. In a lethal force situation eye rakes, throat strikes or grabs, and knee strikes to the groin are all effective options.

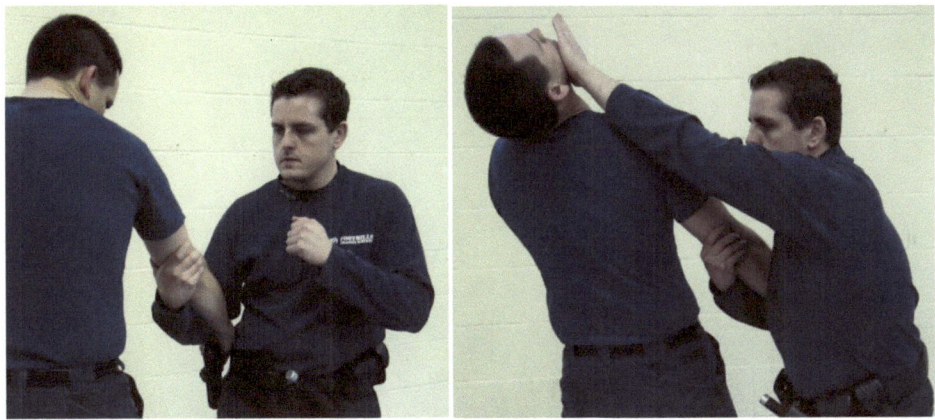

- Once control is established on the arm that attacked, the officers' free arm applies upwards pressure into the jaw of the subject. Simultaneously the officer draws down on the elbow with the grabbing hand and arm. This will force the subject's' eyes up and thereby break their balance to the rear. This position stops the subject from being able to effectively attack and allows the officer to drive in closer to the subject for the Leg Reap Takedown.

Technique #3. Subject Grabs Drawn Sidearm

- The principles in this technique will work for baton also
- First the officer moves their core to their weapon and makes sure it's secured with both hands. In the case of a sidearm maintain regular shooting grip, in the case of a baton grab the tip of the baton

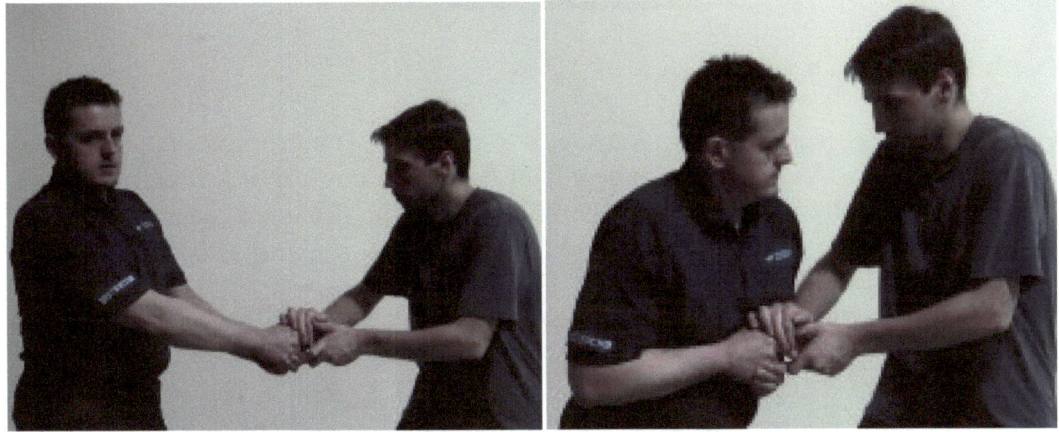

- Next lock the weapon close to the core and rotate in a tight but violent circle. The entire structure rotates the weapon through its circular movement, not the arms.

- If the subject is still holding on strike them with the support hand and repeat in the opposite direction. Repeat until the weapon comes free of their grip.

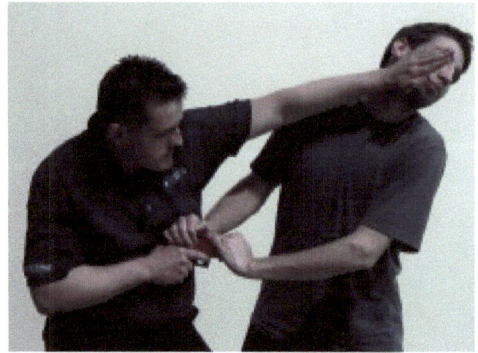

Understanding Weapon Disarming

Weapon disarming is a very dangerous strategy to attempt. The primary danger is to any persons surrounding the event. As an officer and subject fight over control of a firearm the muzzle tends to rotate and point wildly around the two combatants. If the firearm discharges during the incident officers will have little to no control over where the round discharges to.

Secondly while the officer and subject are fighting over the firearm the muzzle might point at the officer when the firearm discharges.

Contrary to popular belief if an automatic firearm discharges while the officer is holding the receiver or slide the chance of injury to their hand is very low. The action of most calibers of firearms can be held closed with hand strength when the round discharges.

Before attempting to disarm a subject an officer must understand these dangers and understand that before even attempting a disarming technique they must be close to the subject, within one arms reach. They must also understand that by attempting a disarming technique their action must be faster than the reaction of the subject. Therefore once an officer makes the decision to act they do so with speed, commitment, and violence.

Technique #4. Rotating Weapon Strips

- The officer moves in towards the subject on a slight angle and moves the gun with their hand.
- Next the officer secures the gun with both hands in a over-under grip and secures it to their core.

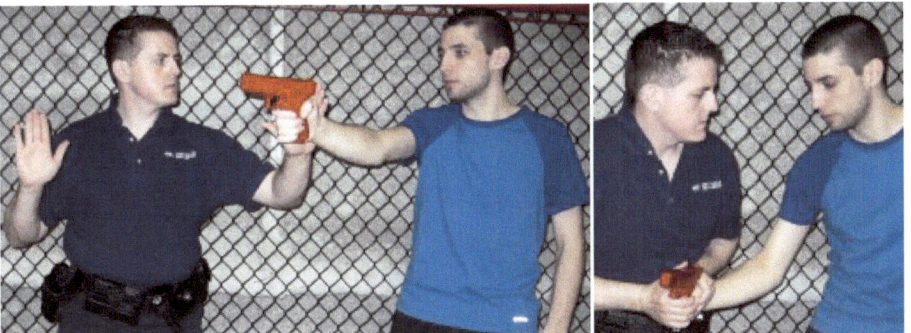

- Finally the officer uses footwork to rotate their hips and shoulders into the subject aiming the muzzle of the firearm at the subject. Once the subject's grip releases on the firearm the officer creates distance and prepares for follow up techniques.

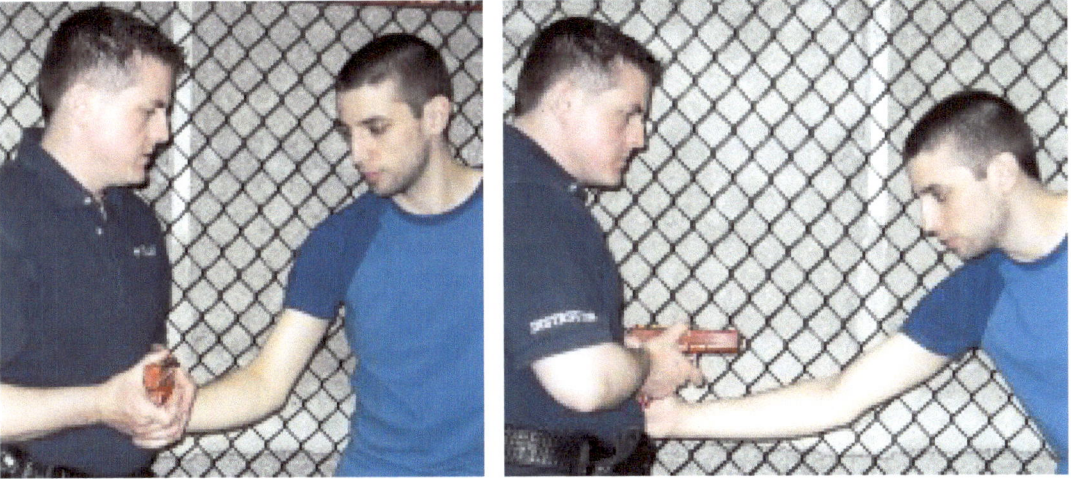

- The same method can be used in the event an officer is being held hostage from behind. Initiate the technique by rotating into the subject while turning to face them and repeat the sequence illustrated above.

Technique #5. Counter Pressure Weapon Strips

- Counter pressure weapon strips work best for disarming a subject of a straight weapon such as a baton or a knife.
  To effectively strip the weapon out of a subject's hand the officer first secures the subject's weapon hand and begins to rotate their wrist either to the outside OR inside.
- With their other hand the officer uses their open palm to apply pressure in the opposite direction of the rotation.

- This type of disarm is most effective when the officer already has control of a subject.

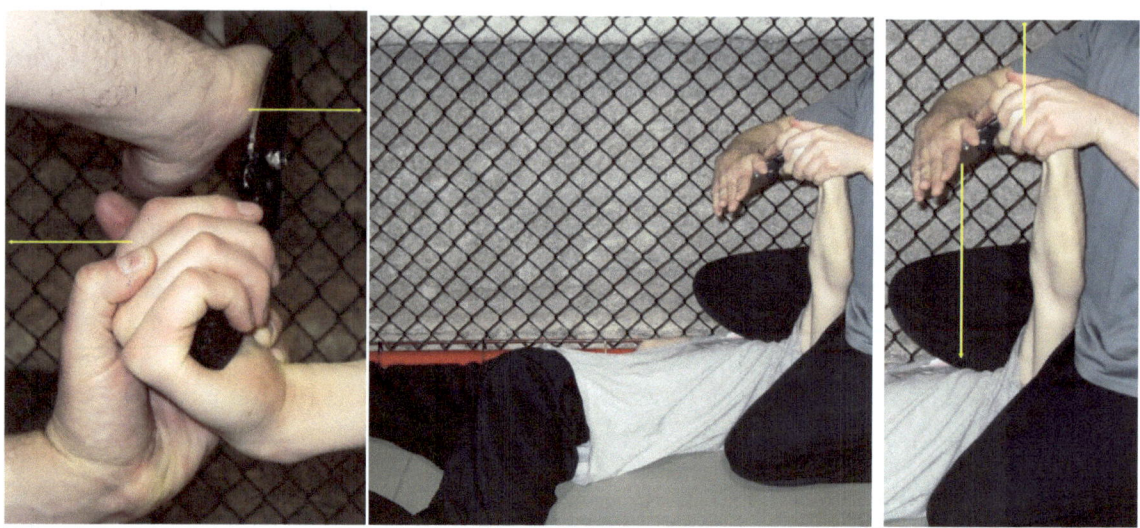

Module 14 Conclusion

If ever weapons are introduced into a combative equation the danger level increases exponentially. Remember that armed officers introduce weapons into EVERY situation because they have weapons and equipment that can be taken from them and either used against them or members of the public.

Officers must understand the details in the techniques regarding retention and disarming, including angles of attack, gripping the weapon, utilizing core and rotational strength, and understanding reaction time. Understanding these principles as well as appreciating the danger of the situation to both the officer and bystanders will help officers understand when their window of opportunity presents itself to attempt a disarm if they ever find themselves in these extremely dangerous situations.

Instructor Notes

Technique #1.

1. Often in the beginning of training students will rush the technique and try to apply downwards pressure on top of their partners hand into the holster or grab their forearm. If the student has already completed the Inside Position Combatives module that should help the students move past this problem. Controlling the pace of the repetitions will also help.

Technique #2.

1. With the cross grab application some students will display a hesitancy to move through the subject and attempt to reach for the leg reap. Watch the students to see if they're leaning back and reaching with their foot for the opposing pressure on the low line.

Technique #3.

1. There are two common mistakes with Technique #3. The first is trying to pull the weapon to the core instead of relying on foot work to move the core to the weapon. And the second is extending the arms making a large circle. Watch students to ensure they're using their core properly and that their entire structure moves the weapon in it's circle.

Technique #4

1. The first error when students attempt to learn the rotating disarm is to not effectively move inside the reactionary gap while redirecting the muzzle of the sidearm. Footwork and handwork should be applied simultaneously not independent of each other.

2. Secondly watch the students to ensure they're establishing the over-under grip. Demonstrate how a subject can pull the firearm out of their grip if the over-under grip isn't established.

3. Watch to make sure that the student is moving their core to the firearm before attempting the body rotation.

4. Lastly watch students to ensure that they're rotating into the subject NOT away from.

Technique #5.

1. Instructors must give students a practical understanding of when to attempt a counter pressure disarm. This is most effectively applied after taking an armed assailant down and disarming them before follow up control is attempted.

Exams and Answer Keys

Control Tactics Written Exam

ANSWER KEY

1. Section 25 of the Canadian Criminal Code states that persons who use force in the enforcement of law are legally justified in doing so so long as the force used was **Reasonable and Necessary** (2 marks)

2. In order to not be found guilty of an assault, force applied during a situation must be reasonable according to the **Totality** of **Circumstances** (2 marks)

3. When determining whether or not force is reasonable the relationship between the **Officer Variables**, **Subject Variables**, and **Circumstantial Variables** are examined. (3 marks)

4. What is the underlying Ethic in FTS Training referred to as and what does it state? (3pts)

   Dual Life Ethic
   Protection of the officers own life
   Protection of Everyone Else's life

5. Fill in the Training Triangle (5 marks)

Training Triangle (top to bottom):
- **Techniques**
- **Body Mechanics**
- **Tactics**
- **Law**
- **Ethics**

6. List 3 factors that influence successful communication with another person. (3 marks)

    Any 3 of;
    - **Language barriers of the parties**
    - **Ethnicity**
    - **Religion**
    - **Gender**
    - **State of mind**
    - **Subject matter**
    - **Level of education**
    - **Level of buy-in to the situation**

7. Once a subject is secured in handcuffs it is the officers responsibility to fit check the handcuffs. T or F. (1 mark) **TRUE**

8. Label the Cranial Pressure Points (5 marks)

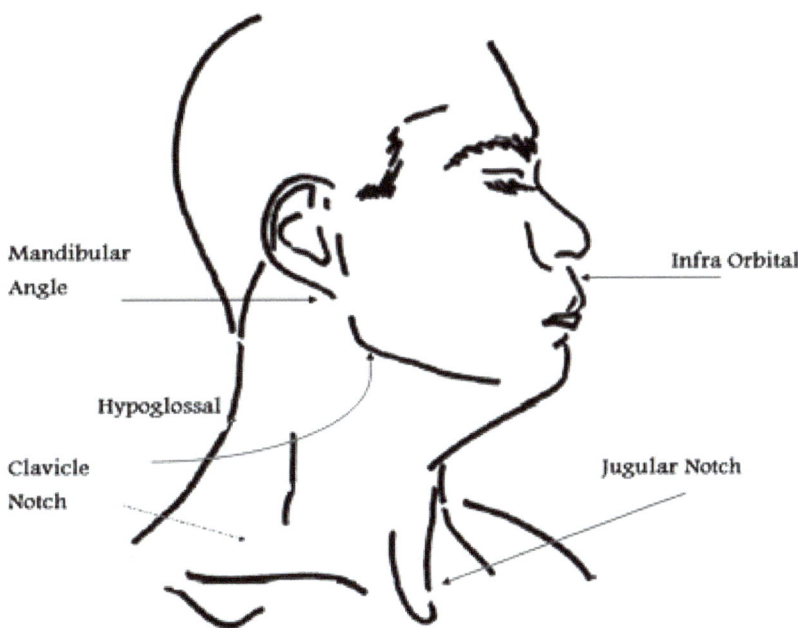

9. The 2 methods of applying pain to pressure points are **Touch Pressure** and **Striking**. (2 marks)

10. Pain Control works because of the Punishment - Reward Principle. T or F. (1 mark) **True**

11. To maximize safety when establishing the Escort Position, where should the officers hands should make initial contact on the subject? (1 mark)

    Elbow

12. List the 3 areas of the body OC has a physiological effect. (3 marks)

    **Respiratory System
    eyes
    skin**

13. List 2 symptoms for each above mentioned areas. (6 marks)

    **Inflammation mucus membranes/mucus secretion
    Coughing/shortness of breath
    Tightness in chest**

    **Painful burning in eyes/tearing/redness/swelling
    Visual impairment/involuntary closure**

    **Burning of skin/pain
    Visible redness/swelling
    Loss of function**

14. A collapsible baton is primarily used in the Open Mode. T or F. (1 mark) **TRUE**

15. Which Strike is the most powerful? (1mark)

    Forehand

16. What is the intended target for a Forehand or Backhand Strike? (1 mark)

    Subject Thigh

17. Blocking strikes are delivered using a slashing motion. T or F (1 mark) **TRUE**

18. When using a baton explain the body mechanic for maximizing power delivery. (3 marks)

    **Hip rotation using the ball of the foot
    Striking with the baton horizontal
    Palm of the weapon hand palm up**

19. When using the baton in the closed mode the thumb is capped over the butt and the strike is delivered with the tip of the baton. T or F (1 mark) **FALSE**

20. A baton is an effective weapon in a deadly force altercation. T or F (1 mark) **FALSE**

21. Balance manipulation is a principle that relies on disrupting the natural homeostatic state between the relationship between the shoulders, hips, knees, and ankles. T or F. (1 mark) **False**

22. List 3 factors that make a Ground Fight very dangerous. (3 marks)

    Any 3 of;
    - **stomping and kicking**
    - **more kinetic energy is delivered from strikes due to counter pressure**
    - **top position can generate more power and use less energy by striking with gravity and body mechanics**
    - **the bottom position quiet often can't reach the person with the top position with strikes due to body mechanics**
    - **limited as to what weapons they can access to control the subject**
    - **officer is on the bottom position they don't have the option of disengagement**
    - **moving on the ground requires more energy to overcome friction**
    - **moving on the ground may cause dirt and debris to become lodged in an officers equipment thereby causing malfunctions or it may tear and rip equipment and remove it from the officers belt**
    - **ability to deal with multiple opponent's is drastically limited**

23. Strikes can be used as an effective method of regaining skeletal alignment and forwards action. T or F. (1 mark) **TRUE**

Control Tactics Written Exam

Name:_____
Date:_____
Class Number:_____
Score:_____/50 = _____%
Examiner:_____

PASS/FAIL

1. Section 25 of the Canadian Criminal Code states that persons who use force in the enforcement of law are legally justified in doing so, so long as the force used was _____ (2 marks)

2. In order to not be found guilty of an assault, force applied during a situation must be reasonable according to the _____ of _____ (2 marks)

3. When determining whether or not force is reasonable the relationship between the _____, _____, and _____ are examined. (3 marks)

4. What is the underlying Ethic in FTS Training referred to as and what does it state? (3pts)

5. Fill in the Training Triangle (5 marks)

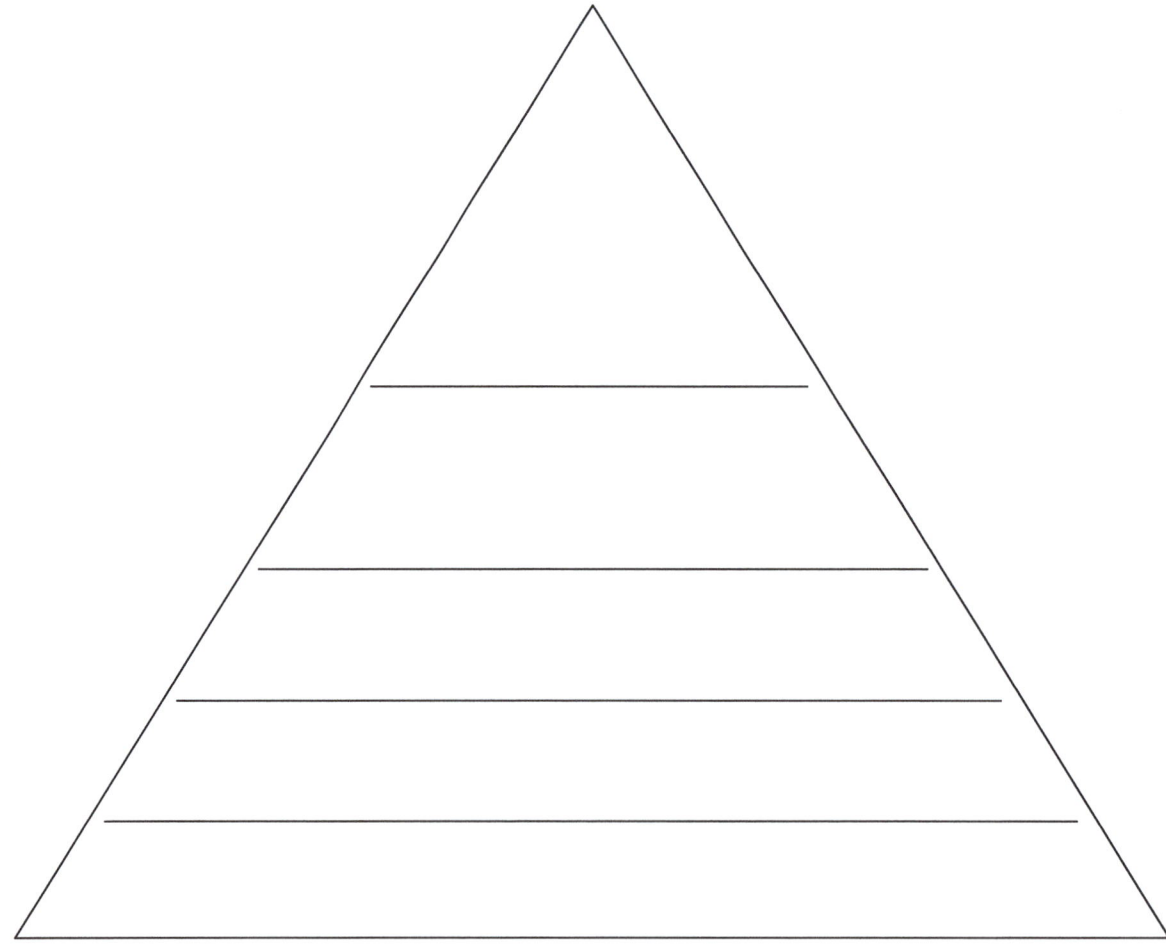

6. List 3 factors that influence successful communication with another person. (3 marks)

7. Once a subject is secured in handcuffs it is the officers responsibility to fit check the handcuffs. T or F. (1 mark)

8. Label the Cranial Pressure Points (5marks)

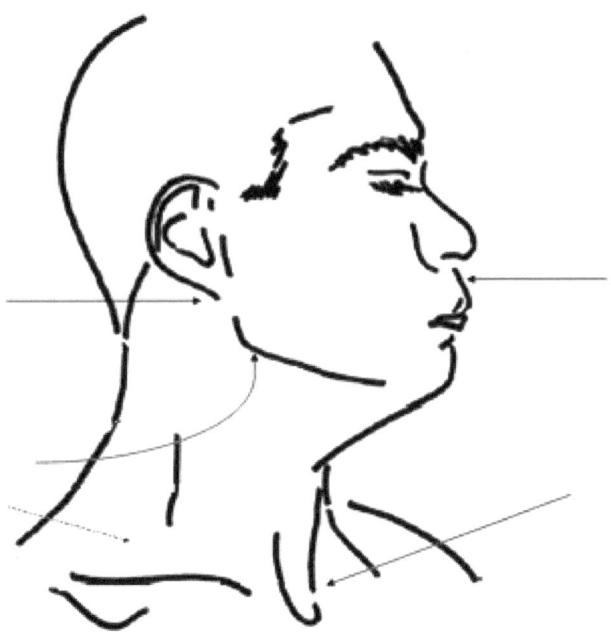

9. The 2 methods of applying pain to pressure points are _____ and _____. (2 marks)

10. Pain Control works because of the Punishment - Reward Principle. T or F. (1 mark)

11. To maximize safety when establishing the Escort Position, where should the officers hands should make initial contact on the subject? (1 mark)

12. List the 3 areas of the body OC has a physiological effect. (3 marks)

13. List 2 symptoms for each above mentioned areas. (6 marks)

14. A collapsible baton is primarily used in the Open Mode. T or F. (1 mark)

15. Which Strike is the most powerful? (1mark)

16. What is the intended target for a Forehand or Backhand Strike? (1 mark)

17. Blocking strikes are delivered using a slashing motion. T or F (1 mark)

18. When using a baton explain the body mechanic for maximizing power delivery. (3 marks)

19. When using the baton in the closed mode the thumb is capped over the butt and the strike is delivered with the tip of the baton. T or F (1 mark)

20. A baton is an effective weapon in a deadly force altercation. T or F (1 mark)

21. Balance manipulation is a principle that relies on disrupting the natural homeostatic state between the relationship between the shoulders, hips, knees, and ankles. T or F. (1 mark)

22. List 3 factors that make a Ground Fight very dangerous. (3 marks)

23. Strikes can be used as an effective method of regaining skeletal alignment and forwards action. T or F. (1 mark)

Control Tactics Practical Exam

Name:_____
Date:_____
Class Number:_____
Score:_____ / _____ = _____ %
Examiner:_____

PASS/FAIL

Name			
Agency			
Date			
Technique	Attempt 1	Attempt 2	Attempt 3

References

A note on references; The techniques and opinions in this manual have been accumulated over the course of 20 years of training with dozens of influential instructors and exposure to their programs. Where possible references are provided to the most influential source or primary source of information for the technique and/or concept.

Module 1

1. HOBAN, Jack. "The Ethical Warrior." ILEETA Conference. Westin Chicago North Shore, Wheeling IL. 2013. Lecture
2. Alberta Sheriffs Control Tactics Manual
3. WALT, Noah. "Contra y contra eskrima." FTS Inc. Okotoks AB. 2013. Demonstrations.
4. "Appendix E: DSM-IV-TR Criteria for Posttraumatic Stress Disorder." *Bookshelf NCBI Resources*. Online. 2013. http://www.ncbi.nlm.nih.gov/books/NBK83241.

Module 3

1. 2010 Martins Annual Criminal Code: Student Edition. Aurora, Ontario: Canada Law Book: A Division of the Cartwright Group Ltd.; 2009.
2. 2010 Martins Annual Criminal Code: Student Edition. Aurora, Ontario: Canada Law Book: A Division of the Cartwright Group Ltd.; 2009.
3. 2010 Martins Annual Criminal Code: Student Edition. Aurora, Ontario: Canada Law Book: A Division of the Cartwright Group Ltd.; 2009.

Module 4

1. O' Malley/Woodford. "PATH Instructor Course." ILEETA Conference. Westin Chicago North Shore, Wheeling IL. 2007. Demonstration.
2. HOBAN, Jack. "Controlling Space." Bujinkan Seminar. Chicago IL. 2013. Demonstration.

Module 5

1. WILLIS, Brian "ACE Knife Defense Instructor Course." Winning Mind Training. Calgary AB. 2004. Demonstration.
2. JOHNS, Chris "Control/Defensive Tactics." Reasonable Use of Force Professional Law Enforcement Training Conference. National Law Enforcement Training Center Kansas City MI. 2012. Demonstration.

Module 6

1. PPCT Inc. DT Inst Manual
2. Gray, Henry. *Anatomy of the Human Body.* Philadelphia: Lea & Febiger, 1918; Bartleby.com, 2000. www.bartleby.com/107/

3. Gray, Henry. *Anatomy of the Human Body.* Philadelphia: Lea & Febiger, 1918; Bartleby.com, 2000. www.bartleby.com/107/
4. Gray, Henry. *Anatomy of the Human Body.* Philadelphia: Lea & Febiger, 1918; Bartleby.com, 2000. www.bartleby.com/107/

Module 7

1. SMITH, Larry "Compliance and Control Holds." ILEETA Conference. Westin Chicago North Shore, Wheeling IL. 2009. Demonstration.
2. SMITH, Larry "Compliance and Control Holds." ILEETA Conference. Westin Chicago North Shore, Wheeling IL. 2009. Demonstration.
3. SMITH, Larry "Compliance and Control Holds." ILEETA Conference. Westin Chicago North Shore, Wheeling IL. 2009. Demonstration.

Module 8

1. BOURGE, Bob. "Defensive Tactics Instructors Course." Alberta Solicitor General Staff Training College, Edmonton AB. 2013. Demonstration.
2. BOURGE, Bob. "Defensive Tactics Instructors Course." Alberta Solicitor General Staff Training College, Edmonton AB. 2013. Demonstration.
3. BOURGE, Bob. "Defensive Tactics Instructors Course." Alberta Solicitor General Staff Training College, Edmonton AB. 2013. Demonstration.
4. SETCAN Corporation. "Oleoresin Capsicum Instructor Training." Alberta Solicitor General Staff Training College, Edmonton AB. 2008. Demonstration.

Module 9

1. SIDDLE, Bruce. PPCT Defensive Tactics Instructor Manual. PPCT Management Systems, Inc. Belleville, IL. 2003.
2. SIDDLE, Bruce. PPCT Defensive Tactics Instructor Manual. PPCT Management Systems, Inc. Belleville, IL. 2003.
3. SIDDLE, Bruce. PPCT Defensive Tactics Instructor Manual. PPCT Management Systems, Inc. Belleville, IL. 2003.
4. BOURGE, Bob. "Defensive Tactics Instructors Course." Alberta Solicitor General Staff Training College, Edmonton AB. 2013. Demonstration.

Module 10

1. MESSINA, Phil. "Combat Physio-Kinetics Instructor Course." ." ILEETA Conference. Westin Chicago North Shore, Wheeling IL. 2007. Demonstration.
2. SIDDLE, Bruce. PPCT Defensive Tactics Instructor Manual. PPCT Management Systems, Inc. Belleville, IL. 2003.
3. BUTLER, Chris. "Lateral Vascular Neck Restraint System Trainer Certification." Calgary Police Service, Calgary AB. 2007. Demonstration.

Module 11

1. BLAUR, Tony. "SPEAR System for Law Enforcement." ." ILEETA Conference. Westin Chicago North Shore, Wheeling IL. 2009. Demonstration.

Module 12

1. BLAUR, Tony. "SPEAR System for Law Enforcement." ." ILEETA Conference. Westin Chicago North Shore, Wheeling IL. 2009. Demonstration.
2. WILLIS, Brian. "W3 Ground Fighting Instructor Course." Winning Mind Training, Calgary AB. 2005. Demonstration.
3. WILLIS, Brian. "W3 Ground Fighting Instructor Course." Winning Mind Training, Calgary AB. 2005. Demonstration.
4. INMAN, Brad "Ground Defense/Control Tactics." Reasonable Use of Force Professional Law Enforcement Training Conference. National Law Enforcement Training Center Kansas City MI. 2012. Demonstration.
5. FULLER, Fletch. "ISR Matrix." ILEETA Conference. Chicago IL. 2013. Demonstration.
6. WILLIS, Brian. "W3 Ground Fighting Instructor Course." Winning Mind Training, Calgary AB. 2005. Demonstration.
7. WILLIS, Brian. "W3 Ground Fighting Instructor Course." Winning Mind Training, Calgary AB. 2005. Demonstration.
8. WILLIS, Brian. "W3 Ground Fighting Instructor Course." Winning Mind Training, Calgary AB. 2005. Demonstration.
9. Gracie Combatives Online Training Curriculum. 2014. Available online http://www.gracieacademy.com/gracie_combatives.asp.
10. KEITH, Kelly. "KINETX Reversible Grip Baton Instructor Course." Westin Chicago North Shore, Wheeling IL.. 2008. Demonstration.

Module 14

1. YOUNG, David. `Handgun Retention Instructor.`` ILEETA Conference. Westin Chicago North Shore, Wheeling IL.. 2010. Demonstration.
2. GREGORY, Anthony. `Weapon Retention and Disarm Instructor Course. Westin Chicago North Shore, Wheeling IL.. 2008. Demonstration.
3. SIDDLE, Bruce. PPCT Defensive Tactics Instructor Manual. PPCT Management Systems, Inc. Belleville, IL. 2003.
4. HUNCAR, Joel. `Weapon Disarm Principles.` Ft. Steele BC. 2010. Demonstration.

www.ingramcontent.com/pod-product-compliance
Lightning Source LLC
Chambersburg PA
CBHW060813010526
44117CB00002B/20